Teachers' Professional Responsibilities

Teachers' Professional Responsibilities

Frances Spackman

David Fulton Publishers
London
Published in association with the Roehampton Institute

David Fulton Publishers Ltd
2 Barbon Close, Great Ormond Street, London WC1N 3JX

First published in Great Britain by
David Fulton Publishers, 1991

Note: The right of Frances Spackman to be identified as the author of this work
has been asserted by her in accordance with the Copyright, Designs and Patents
Act 1988.

British Library Cataloguing in Publication Data

Spackman, Frances
  Teachers' professional responsibilities
  I. Title
  371.10023

  ISBN 1-85346-162-8

Typeset by Chapterhouse, Formby L37 3PX
Printed in Great Britain by
BPCC Wheaton Ltd. Exeter.

Contents

Introduction vii

1 Initial Formalities 1

2 Health and Safety 9

3 Teachers' Unions 13

4 Staffroom Relationships 19

5 Teachers and Parents 29

6 Out of School 43

7 Teachers and Pupils 55

8 Professional Development 73

9 Personal Matters 83

Further Reading 100

Index 101

Introduction

Every new teacher needs to be self-reliant and to understand the extent of their legal and professional responsibilities. This book is intended to bridge the gap between the accumulated 'know how' which teachers acquire gradually and the serious legal advice which is provided by a solicitor. One hesitates to suggest meeting trouble half-way or to worry people who already have enough anxiety to cope with, so it is in the spirit of 'forewarned is forearmed' that the book is written. There are many pitfalls which may beset teachers, whether they are novices or experienced staff. This has always been the case but is even more true with the increasing amount of legislation which applies to many aspects of education.

My intention in this book is to pass on some guidance and help for teachers who are beginning their careers or who are returning to teaching. In either case, enormous changes in schools and in teaching will be noticed. Time was when teachers, having trained, were initiated into the profession simply by being in contact with experienced colleagues and perhaps by belonging to a union. The pace of day-to-day activity in school used to be sufficiently unhurried to allow new teachers to observe and learn and to enable established staff to guide them when necessary, but this is now rarely the case.

Much of the advice offered here is born of experience and so it may be rather anecdotal in places. The truly great horror stories are left to the wags in the staff room who have the advantage of local authenticity being 'in situ'. The major, overwhelming problems, matters which call for expert advice, will not feature in this book; its scope is confined to guidance and reassurance rather than the tackling of complex legal matters.

The professional and legal responsibilities of teachers, such as the duty of care which they owe to children, remain fairly constant over time. Some, however, emerge as a result of a major change in Government policy, as with teachers' contracts of employment. Other responsibilities evolve in response to particular current incidents highlighted in the media, as with the regulations now governing school trips.

Any new teacher who keeps up with the debates on education which are aired in the media will find it all the easier to contribute to discussions inside and outside the staffroom. Experienced teachers often expect the newest recruits to the profession to be well informed when, in reality, new staff may be the very people who feel quite inadequate and ill-prepared. Yet entrants to the profession owe it to themselves to find out exactly what their responsibilities are and what expectations people have of them.

On teaching practice you will have had various opportunities to see what a teacher's lot really is. Also your impression of teachers who taught you at school will still be vivid; they may even have been the initial stimulus for your career choice. When I interview graduates who apply for a PGCE place, there is invariably mention of a particularly significant teacher who was instrumental in sowing the seeds of enthusiasm which had a lasting effect on the applicant. If you have had positive, happy experiences as a pupil – or if you have been on the receiving end of both good and bad teaching, which is more likely to be the case – you need to hold on to those feelings since this will enable you to appreciate what is happening to the children you will be teaching yourself. This is important even if you see very little similarity between yourself as a child and your pupils, or if your experiences seem to differ fundamentally from theirs.

Your teaching practice will have added another dimension. It forms a sort of half-way house where you will have been behind the scenes, as well as trying your hand at the actual work. You will have observed teachers not only engaged in their public performances but also in the staffroom scrambles and last minute panics with the photocopier. You will also have gained an insight into what sort of life teachers lead. What you gather from what you hear and observe will not amount to more than a general impression and, of course, teachers can be quite different 'in real life'. Their home circumstances will obviously have an impact on their approach to work and vice versa. Nevertheless, you will have been able from all this to see which aspects of being a teacher would apply to your own particular circumstances and which would be relevant to your own life and work.

The teachers you meet in your first post will obviously have an effect on you when you start teaching especially since their approval, whether you like it or not, will affect the way you work. Teachers do not work in a vacuum, and even in the most traditional settings, where they might seem to be isolated in their classrooms, the context of the school environment has a considerable impact on their work. If after all you do not feel happy in your school, if the atmosphere is petty or paranoid and you find colleagues difficult to respect or like, then do not stay too long. Some people recommend moving on from a first appointment within a couple of years in any case, in order to leave mistakes behind. I would recommend staying while you feel you are learning your craft and enjoying your teaching. Move on when you think you might be getting jaded or stale.

Whatever happens, you will probably get off to a better start than if you had been trained in the sixties as I was. Then the training of teachers did not include much in the way of classroom management skills or any particular attempt to equip teachers to cope with discipline problems. One was therefore rather at the mercy of the pupils and survival was very much a matter of strength of character and good luck. As a probationary teacher, I was given a seventh stream class of fifteen-year-old school leavers who came to school equipped only with their shiny black handbags containing steel combs for self defence and for backcombing their beehive hair-dos. It could not happen now, but then I had no syllabus, no exam to prepare for, no accountability, no record keeping and absolutely no guidance whatsoever.

The attendance register was the most telling performance indicator for a teacher in those days, at least in my school. It was a stark case of learning to teach without a safety net: decidedly not to be recommended. Once, after a particularly gruelling day, I happened to meet the head and took the opportunity to explain, quite reasonably I thought, that I was scarcely qualified to teach this group of what we then called 'remedial' young adults. 'Well none of us is, dear' was the signal to get on with it.

Now it all seems preposterous, but at the time, although there were many battles, I do remember that there were lots of laughs. I had tremendous, heady freedom to teach what the children seemed to need to know. This was not a bad training ground for developing creative, relevant courses; not a bad training ground either for teaching in the most persuasive and compelling way that one could muster. Yet in spite of all the freedom and independence I experienced in that whacky, exhilarating set up, I am happier now to know that new teachers are better prepared for life in schools during their training and that they receive the sound professional support they need when they get there.

Acknowledgements

I would like to thank Jim Docking for his most generous help and also Rosemary Roscoe, Clare Mason and Louise Walsh for their comments and encouragement.

CHAPTER 1

Initial Formalities

In your initial teacher training course you may have had, in the final stages, general careers advice, including practical help with CVs and perhaps even mock interviews. This can give you valuable interview experience and probably increase your confidence. Students at this stage are wiser than their tutors in knowing the state of the job market through discussions with fellow candidates and the experience of completing job applications.

First appointment

The likelihood is that the sort of school which appeals to you will have become apparent through your teaching practice and that you will therefore have targeted your applications accordingly. At a time of teacher shortage you are likely to be able to be selective, the more so if your subject specialism is in short supply. Some local education authorities are offering probationary teachers considerable inducements and 'golden hellos' as they vie with each other in order to attract staff.

Until recently it was unusual to pay newly qualified teachers from the time of their appointment, so that they would begin work at the end of the Summer term rather than the beginning of September. Now this practice is more common. No-one becomes a teacher for the perks, so when something comes along which is close to resembling a good offer, it is not to be sneezed at. Newly qualified teachers are likely to be at their most geographically mobile, so it is worth a wide-ranging look to see what is available, whether it be help with accommodation, summer employment, a cash sum, attractive

loan schemes or even assistance towards a mortgage. These inducements are entirely dependent on the teacher supply situation, so they
will not necessarily be repeated each year. However, you may be able
to negotiate your position on the pay scale.

While no-one would want to pour cold water on what looks like a
happy position for probationers, there is another cautionary note to
sound. Anyone who is offered a first appointment in a secondary
school in charge of a department on their own should be careful. It
may be flattering, you may have an easy interview but there are other
things to think about. You need, as a probationer, to be able to rely
on the guidance and support of an experienced head of department.
A head might put pressure on a good young candidate by suggesting
that there would be plenty of independence and freedom to organise
the subject area. Promotion prospects might also be mentioned. No
amount of independence will compensate, however, for the extra
responsibilities involved, or having missed the chance to work with
colleagues who share the same subject specialism. Proper job
descriptions are now automatically part and parcel of the process of
school appointments and they should be both detailed and accurate.
It is reassuring too if the job advertisement explains carefully
beforehand exactly what the job entails. If it matches the picture of
the post which later emerges, this too increases your confidence in the
organisation.

It can be disconcerting if, when you attend an interview, you
discover that the job also entails teaching your second or even third
subject, something which had not been made clear until then. Think
about this possibility and decide beforehand how you will want to
respond. It is worse if such a situation emerges only when the ink is
dry on your contract and your timetable arrives in the post with the
bad news only days before the term begins.

For your own peace of mind it is therefore worth making sure that
you understand the full scope of your teaching commitments before
you accept an appointment. Make sure first of all that you find out
whether your appointment is permanent or for a fixed term. Fixed
term contracts are a fairly recent phenomenon and, as a new teacher,
you may not feel that you can accept a position on those terms since
security and continuity are especially important for beginners.

Interviews

If the experiences of my PGCE students are anything to go by, interviews for first appointments can range from the grand formal occasion at which several competing candidates face a row of governors, to the casual chat with an individual member of staff as you look around the school. Regardless of the degree of formality, an interview is a daunting prospect for which you should prepare well in order to do justice to yourself.

The 'Escape Committee' at my last school (a group of becalmed staff who wanted promotion and who saw no possibility of advancement without moving to another school) demonstrated a variety of approaches to job interviews. Some of the 'Committee' used to do their interview homework thoroughly by finding out as much as they could about the school and its policies and systems. The *Times Educational Supplement* was read assiduously and endless questions and answers were prepared and rehearsed before being put to the test in mock interviews given by fellow 'escapees'.

At the other end of the scale were the spontaneous characters who took the view that they would just be themselves and if that wasn't good enough, then the job would probably not have suited them anyhow. These days however, only secondary Maths, Physics and Modern Language teachers can really afford this degree of confidence.

Pooled experiences from our informal debriefing sessions were invaluable sources of information (as well as therapy), and although individual experiences cannot be replicated exactly, the confidence and support gained from the sharing of tips and 'know how' was as useful as the impressive bank of information we accumulated.

New teachers need to prepare carefully for interviews. Since they will not have much experience to fall back on, they must rely instead on being well-informed in their subject area and its place in the National Curriculum; they should be able to articulate a sound philosophy of education including a view about the principles and practice of equal opportunities and providing for special educational needs; and they should be able to give a good account of their interests and abilities. While it is unlikely that you will be embarrassed by questions which are now forbidden by law, such as asking a young woman when she intends to start a family, you should be alert to the more indirect versions of the same enquiry posed by disingenuous governors. Interviewers are simply not allowed to ask about marital status, religious or political affiliation, or union membership. Candidates for interview can also legally complain if they think that they have been discriminated against on grounds of sex, race or ethnic or national origins, and the governors may then have to appear before an Industrial Tribunal.

Most Heads these days give debriefing interviews. This is an offer to be seized upon because it helps to inform you about your performance as well as providing reassurance on your strong points and giving specific suggestions about where you went wrong and how to correct it.

Contracts

Following the introduction of Local Management of Schools (LMS), and the general financial constraints in the education service, I have been saying to my students who are applying for teaching posts that, whether or not they are professionally any good, at least they are cheap! This is a kind of grim encouragement when interviews are looming, but would be precious little comfort to more established teachers, anxious about the recent changes in the pay regulations and the effect which these will have on the job market and their promotion prospects.

All newly recruited teachers will be aware of the wider responsibilities which schools' governing bodies have for the employment of staff especially now that they also have control over their budgets. The LEA must now appoint the teacher selected by the governors though the job of selection may be delegated. Remember that, even if you are not actually interviewed by anyone other than the headteacher, your obligations as an employee are to the Board of Governors. You will have a contract which sets out formally the basic conditions to which both parties agree and which is largely governed by the Teachers' Pay and Conditions Act 1987. This concerns the exercise of teachers' professional duties. In addition to teaching, it includes other duties which will be allocated by the Head who is legally responsible for directing how each teacher's time is spent. These activities will include such duties as lesson preparation, covering for absent staff, attendance at staff meetings, helping with course development, carrying out assessment and compiling reports, communicating with parents, attending to the progress and welfare of pupils conducting public examinations and participating in appraisal schemes.

It is important to read your contract carefully and not sign your agreement automatically. You will be bound by what you have agreed to. It is unlikely that you will be so preoccupied with the fine print that you challenge there and then the conditions which are presented to you; nevertheless, you should become familiar with them.

You should also realise that, in addition to the terms set out in the contract, there are implied terms which incorporate the reasonable expectations that an employer has of a member of the teaching profession. An example of this might be an understanding that you would not undertake additional employment which might interfere with your teaching. Running in-service work for which payment is made can fall into this rather grey area, since it means that you are being paid twice for the same period. Sometimes this is allowed, however, since there are benefits to be gained for all concerned and it reflects well upon the school. Beware of anything such as making a blatant public criticism of your school's policy which might be regarded as a breach of contract. The relationship which you have with your employer quite properly includes an element of loyalty.

Conditions of work

The letter which you receive confirming your appointment will probably refer to three sets of regulations, copies of which will be available at your school or your local education office. These are:

(a) Regulations of the Department of Education and Science.
(b) Regulations governing the appointment, resignation, suspension and dismissal and other Conditions of Service of Teachers in Nursery, Primary, Secondary and Special Schools.
(c) The Articles of Government of the School.

Over a period of time there may be variations in the terms of these conditions and your employer is obliged to notify you if this should occur. There may also be suggestions which amount to conditions of work which arise during the course of your interview and to which you may give your verbal consent. ('We hope that you will be able to take the Junior Choir under your wing', is an example of this sort of thing.)

Other conditions become established almost by default in the course of your actual employment and are not stated in detail in the standard contract. Undoubtedly some things you will take on willingly and others you may resist. You will also be aware of the difference between an additional responsibility which applies to all members of staff, such as a request that staff escort their classes off the premises at home time, and something you are asked to do as an individual. The latter is much more difficult for a new and therefore vulnerable member of staff. The only way to cope with creeping extra responsibilities is to be firm. People do understand the pressures new staff are under but they sometimes need to be reminded.

Bear in mind that these pressures do not all necessarily emanate from above. An intensive course in assertiveness may be needed if you feel that you are easily put upon and if you have not already covered this aspect of personal management as part of your professional preparation.

It is worth pointing out too that, having verbally accepted a post offered in an interview, it is not reasonable then to renege on your agreement, though legally you are within your rights to do so. Even if you are not formally accused of breach of contract, your name will be mud in the very circles in which you will probably wish to be well regarded.

One of my students was put under considerable pressure at an interview recently to make a decision there and then about the post she was being offered. She stuck to her guns, explained her reservations, and was later congratulated for not allowing herself to be bullied into a premature decision. This is a better course of action than to accept a position and then change your mind afterwards.

Further information

Any written material which is given to you such as a staff handbook, school prospectus or local authority policy statement must be regarded as significant information relating to your employment. Read it carefully and then reread it some weeks later when you have a clearer picture of things. Some of the information you are given will be absolutely vital for your personal welfare, for instance the procedures to follow when you are ill and unable to get to school.

There will be plenty of information outlining your pay and conditions and explaining details of pension schemes and superannuation. If there seems little pressing need to tackle all of these matters right away, at least keep everything in a safe place and award yourself the peace of mind which comes from the certain knowledge that nothing of importance has been thrown away. This particularly applies to such remote matters as superannuation. The Employment Protection (Consolidated) Act 1978 obliges your employer to give you a written statement of your conditions of employment at some time within the first three months of your first term.

Under the Education Reform Act (1988) Local Management of Schools legislation, governing bodies will assume certain powers previously belonging to local education authorities. Pay awards are thus complicated by the fact that governing bodies now have greater discretion in offering incremental enhancement above the standard scale, although LEA guidelines remain.

If you have any nagging doubts about aspects of your work and contract, don't just worry about it. Seek clarification from a reliable source e.g. the Clerk to the Governors or the Head. A telephone call to the staffing section of the Education Department of your local authority should be enough to clear up most technical queries.

You might feel that your enquiry is too trivial or too slight to trouble your employer. If casual reassurance is all that is needed, you can consult the member of staff responsible for your induction or anyone on the staff you have begun to know. If you are still not happy and cannot get satisfaction, you may need to consult a union for some impartial advice but this would be a rather drastic step for someone who is starting out as a teacher. In reality, people are likely to be bending over backwards to help you and ensure that you have as smooth an introduction to teaching as possible.

When you take up your first appointment, the likelihood is that you will be looking forward to meeting your colleagues and pupils and excited at the prospect of putting your prepared programmes into action. The initial formalities of contract and conditions of service are important to the extent that you need to feel secure and well organised but, though it may loom large at the time, once the administrative process is complete you can consider yourself safely on board and able to concentrate on your teaching. (As long as your pay slip arrives, all should be well!)

CHAPTER 2

Health and Safety

Health and Safety legislation has had an impact on the professional responsibilities of teachers in a variety of ways. It both protects teachers as employees and affects them in the exercise of their duties. As a professional duty, a teacher is expected to safeguard pupils' health and safety while they are in school. This applies both to what teachers do and what they fail to do. Negligence can be found if a teacher instructs a child to do something dangerous and equally if he or she forgets to give a warning and an accident occurs as a result. The essential point is the existence of the duty of care which binds all teachers.

There are two main statutory obligations on teachers in this respect; these are set out in the Education (School Teachers' Pay and Conditions of Employment) Order 1987.

One is the obligation to promote the general progress and well-being of the pupils. The other is the duty of maintaining good order and discipline among pupils and the safeguarding of their health and safety. These apply both when pupils are authorised to be on school premises and when they are engaged in authorised activities outside school.

As well as this overall and continual responsibility, there are particular areas of the school which need to be especially well guarded or supervised. Each department will be equipped with the relevant Health and Safety advice. You will probably also come across the DES Safety Series booklets in the staffroom. 'Out of school' activities are also included in a teacher's responsibility and thus will be dealt with in Chapter 6. Some of the likeliest trouble spots are the common areas such as playgrounds, corridors and cloakrooms. Supervision of these places usually falls to the lot of those who are on break duty, a responsibility which you must take very seriously indeed. Never mind the temptation to sneak away early to grab your richly deserved coffee in the staff room and never mind the last minute photocopying which you need for your next lesson; you simply must carry out your break duty at all costs.

Health and safety committee

Each school will have a Health and Safety representative perhaps heading a committee or a group to share the responsibility and report to the Head. Each school, too, will have a policy document on Health and Safety for guidance. Everyone who works in a school should accept some responsibility for conditions and practices in this regard either as they are personally affected or as they observe potential dangers for others.

Health and safety is receiving some long overdue attention in schools and it is in everyone's interest to co-operate with any efforts which are made to improve matters.

Looking at it optimistically, this should have the effect of improving the quality of life for everyone and the working conditions of staff in particular. In schools many unpredictable incidents occur; therefore it is as well to make strenuous efforts to eliminate any which can possibly be foreseen. None of the staff in my last school anticipated the antics of a group of would-be circus performers who 'borrowed' a huge mat after sports day and used it to land on as they hurled themselves out of a first floor window. Great fun was had until someone broke their jaw and landed, this time, in hospital. Steps were then taken to ensure that the performance was never repeated.

Accidents

All schools have procedures which apply in the event of an accident and a named person who is responsible for dealing with cases of illness and any accidents which may happen. There are strict limits now on the remedies which may be dispensed at school.

The more an individual teacher knows about first aid, the more confident he or she is likely to be in an emergency. I went on an excellent St. John's Ambulance course for just this reason but I discovered that your skills become rusty unless they are put into practice, so it is important to know who to call as well as what to do.

Obviously, when individual cases arise and the law is put to the test, particular circumstances are crucial, and the specific details prevent generalisation beyond the counsel of perfection which insists that every care is taken. Being *in loco parentis* means being in place of a parent – a daunting prospect when multiplied by thirty or so, but an important principle on which the welfare of children in school is based. The numbers of parents who have recourse to the law when they consider that they have a claim for negligence is increasing and is bound to increase further. Just as certain is the continuing supply of children who do crazy things which cause accidents and also those who are blameless and still come a cropper. Staff have always had to protect every hair of their charge's heads, as well as their own backs in the process.

In order to protect pupils and staff there are many insurance schemes which cover such things as sports injuries, and for your own peace of mind you should find out exactly how you are covered and in what ways your pupils are protected. In the first instance you can discuss this with the person responsible for you as a probationer. Union representatives will have this information as will the member of staff responsible for Health and Safety. Often too the school secretary can point you in the direction of the relevant policy. You should make it your business to check on this, and sooner rather than later.

CHAPTER 3

Teachers' Unions

Joining a union

There are six teachers' unions, two of which are particularly for headteachers and deputy heads. It is quite likely that you will already have been approached with an invitation to join one of the other four associations – AMMA, NAS/UWT, NUT and PAT (see table 3.1).

As a new teacher you have to decide whether or not to join a union or professional association and if so, which one to join. Essentially you will need to have a clear idea of how you would wish to be represented, if at all, as a professional teacher. If you are particularly interested you can send for the literature produced by each union so that you can compare their policies and the benefits which they offer.

In addition you will be aware of the union activity which takes place at the school where you are working. Since union membership involves joining together in order to benefit from effective representation, you need to find out which unions operate in your staffroom and which have the greatest support among those teachers with whom you feel you have most in common. Find out who the union representatives are. This is quite a useful yardstick when you are making up your mind.

In the same way that your religious and political allegiances are your own concern, your membership (or non-membership) of a union is also your own business. It would be naive to suppose, though, that these matters go unnoticed by your employers, especially at a time of any teacher union activity or industrial action; and there may well come a point at which your loyalties are severely tested.

Table 3.1 Teachers' Unions

Assistant Masters and Mistresses Association (A.M.M.A.) 7 Northumberland Street, London WC2N 5DA
National Association of Schoolmasters/Union of Women Teachers (N.A.S./U.W.T.) Hillscourt Education Centre, Rose Hill, Birmingham B45 8RS
National Union of Teachers (N.U.T.) Hamilton House, Mabledon Place, London WC1H 9BD
Professional Association of Teachers (P.A.T.) 99 Friary Gate, Derby DE1 1EZ

If you keep a weather eye on the *Times Educational Supplement*, you will gain an idea of the state of the teachers' unions and how their fortunes are waxing and waning. This will help you to gain an objective view to balance the effects of the promotional materials which you may receive.

Disputes

There are times when union membership simply provides the security of belonging to an organisation which will bail you out if you get into trouble. At other times when there are serious issues which have an impact on all teachers you may regard the representation of your interests as a matter of grave importance. Teachers as an occupational group have never had a sparkling reputation as union negotiators. Apart from anything else there has never been a single voice behind which to unite. Possible amalgamations of unions may alter this state of affairs.

Among school staffs, difficulties and disputes can and do occur in stressful times relating to both internal and external matters. Problems can be compounded if more than one union is involved and if they vary in their approaches. Staffroom disputes can become acrimonious if there are inter-union tensions, especially if the successful action of one union is dependent on the support, whether active or passive, of the others. While you might expect a rift perhaps to be exploited by senior management, it is surprising how sympathetic Heads often are. They value highly the existence of a harmonious and united staff and are anxious therefore to work with the unions.

Teachers' morale

Morale in the teaching profession is an important matter. Nationally
it receives much attention when teacher vacancies cannot be filled,
when staff turnover is high and also when surveys reveal that many
trained teachers are leaving the profession. At a local level conditions
can vary: there may well be a happier picture here, and you should
judge for yourself. The functioning of the union in your school may
give an indication of employee/employer relationships. If nothing
much seems to be happening, it could be due to apathy or it could be
due to harmony. If the unions seem to be very active, it could mean
either healthy involvement or it might indicate tension and conflict.
In the long run much will depend on the quality of the school
management and the relationships among the staff which in turn will
be reflected in the way unions work.

Union services

The range of services which are provided by the teachers' unions is
considerable. You may have had an indication of these in the
literature which some unions produce for student teachers.
Admittedly it is part of their recruitment effort, but nevertheless it
shows the scope of what they provide.

In order to find out exactly what is on offer, ring or write to the
associations and make comparisons. You must do this in relation to
your particular needs, of course, since an impressive array of benefits
will be no more use than a row of beans if they are not relevant to
your situation. For a comprehensive outline of the benefits and
services offered by all six unions see table 3.2.

These services fall into the following general categories:

(1) *Services common to all unions*

- Legal protection with specialist legal advice available with
  particular attention paid to those areas which are relevant to the
  professional needs of teachers.
- Free occupational insurance covering categories such as personal
  accident and malicious damage to cars.
- Car insurance in the form of policies tailor-made for teachers.
- Professional advice and support.

Table 3.2 What they offer

SHA	PAT	NUT	NAS UWT	NAHT	AMMA		
✓	✓	✓	✓	✓	✓	Legal help - (Professional matters)	
	✓	✓	✓	✓		(Personal matters)	
N/A	N/A	£100 WEEK	N/A	N/A	N/A	Hospital benefit	⎫
£5000	N/A	£7500	£3000	£4000	£2500	Personal accident	Free
N/A	£108	£135	£150	£100	£135	Personal property	occupational insurance
£50	£75	£45	£75	£150	£65	Malicious damage to vehicles	
£1M	£1M	1	£1.5M	£½M	£1M	Personal liability	⎭
✓		2	✓	✓	✓	Non-contributory benefit fund	
		2	✓			Low-cost retirement home	
✓						Help with school purchasing	
9		8	12	9	8	Magazine/Newsletter per year	
✓	✓	✓		✓	✓	Independent financial advice	
	✓	✓	✓	✓	✓	Credit card at preferential rates	
✓	✓	✓	✓	✓	✓	Insurance (General)	⎫
				✓	✓	Insurance (Medical)	
✓			✓	✓	✓	Home loans	
✓	✓	✓	✓		✓	Personal loans	Discounts
✓	✓	✓	✓	✓	✓	Car purchase	
✓	✓	✓			✓	Car hire	
✓	✓	✓	✓	3	✓	General goods and travel	⎭

1 The NUT says its legal help scheme makes this unnecessary.
2 The NUT runs the Teachers Benevolent Fund which runs retirement homes + gives help to members and non-members.
3 Travel only
From Times Educational Supplement, March 29, 1991

(2) *Services provided by some unions*

- Home finance and mortages can be secured through some unions.
- Several unions run travel companies.
- Financial services and loans are a provision supplied by some unions.
- Some unions provide courses and opportunities for professional development.

Other matters to be considered are the ease of access to whatever facilities and services you might use. The existence of a convenient local branch, for instance, might sway your choice. The level of union subscriptions varies and although there are lower rates for probationary teachers, the standard rate is the one to judge by since you are unlikely to chop and change unions after your probationary year, unless something untoward happens.

While shopping around you might look carefully at how policies vary on different issues. You might be interested too in the leadership of the unions and the way they are run. Although on a practical level you may be interested in getting value for your money, the really important concern is that your interests as a professional teacher are being protected and that your views are being represented effectively.

Union politics

Current events and the responses of the unions will undoubtedly influence your attitude to the various unions but you also need to be aware of their individual policies and philosophy. Find out, for example, about each union's views on strike action. This is a more sensible plan than joining an organisation only to find out later that you are not happy to withdraw your labour when called upon to do so. You need to be quite certain in your own mind about how you view industrial action. What stand would you take personally if required to participate in, for example, ballots, working to rule, withdrawal of labour, demonstrating, joining in marches? How would you wish to be represented should any of these matters arise?

You may have seen reports in the press of further merger discussions between some of the teachers' unions. At present there are differences in policy and philosophy which may prove too great to be overcome so nothing may come of it. There is a decline in membership numbers, however, which makes it quite likely that some amalgamations will take place. There are certainly major

changes afoot which will affect the arrangements for pay determination machinery, pension arrangements, contracts and so on and
the stance of the unions will play a significant part in their resolution.
Local pay agreements may lead to fragmentation and thus the
weakening of the unions' voices in national negotiations. This in itself
may make it all the more vital to ensure strong union protection for
individual teachers.

If you do your homework thoroughly and find yourself in the
professional association with which you identify most readily you
may find that it turns out to be not merely a matter of protecting your
back but a very positive dimension to your working life.

CHAPTER 4
Staffroom Relationships

Joining the staff

The extent to which, as a new teacher, you fit into the staffroom and feel at ease with your colleagues may mean the difference between being happy at work or downright miserable. It is as much a matter of luck as of judgement. However carefully you try to size up the school you apply to, you are unable to tell with certainty what it would actually be like to work there. Human relationships are unpredictable and the behaviour of groups can be fickle. While acknowledging that joining an established group can have its problems, there are ways in which you can make a successful debut more likely. A newcomer can contribute with a positive and enthusiastic attitude to any staff however settled a group they may seem at first glance. It is most important to realise that teachers' professional relationships are both formal and informal. These will inevitably overlap in practice and, equally inevitably, the grey area is often where problems arise. All school staffs are different. Even two schools organised on the same lines will still have very different staffroom groups by reason of the human factors involved.

These points are obviously general but nevertheless important. As a new teacher you will have had teaching practice which will have provided you with an inkling of staff dynamics, but from an outsider's perspective. Granted the observer sees most of the game, but this is scant preparation for 'real life' when you arrive in the staffroom on your first day. Initial teacher training courses, while they will stress the importance of teacher-pupil relationships, are unlikely to delve into professional relationships to a marked extent,

19

unless a problem arises on teaching practice. On the whole, these matters do not loom large until you begin work.

In the staffroom

The staffroom has a very special function in a school. Not only is it a meeting place, a sanctuary and a place for relaxation; it is also a professional forum for discussion and debate, in fact a key setting for the induction and development of newcomers, both formally and informally. The organisation of a school is invariably hierarchical and new teachers quickly see that their place in the scheme of things, like it or lump it, is likely to be near the bottom. However democratic, the staffroom too has its own informal but tangible pecking order. It is in the staffroom particularly that the staff will be, or should be, seen working as a team and this must be borne in mind by new staff. While there is always a welcome for a new teacher, it is inevitably accompanied by a whole set of expectations, some of which cannot be met immediately, even by the most accomplished new teacher. There may be anxieties, for example, that a newly qualified teacher will be a 'passenger' through lack of experience. On the other hand, a real or imagined threat might be perceived in the form of an energetic, well qualified enthusiast.

Staff may assume that a newcomer is keen to become involved in extra-curricular activities, and indeed this may well be the case. New staff are valued for their enthusiasm and energy, and new teachers are right to seize an opportunity to make a contribution to the life of the school. A balance must be struck, however, between putting maximum effort into the main task for which the teacher has been employed, and getting involved in additional activities which may jeopardise the main work in the classroom. Feel free to insist on managing your own time. An overview on the matter will be taken by the teacher responsible for new staff, your head of department perhaps, but you also have a personal responsibility for exercising judgement. 'Directed time' which has been mentioned already could be seen as having a protective function in this instance.

Staffroom etiquette

Staffroom etiquette is often a source of frustration for newcomers, yet it is not something to take lightly. Obviously it is possible to place too much importance on the perceived foibles of fellow members of staff, but they can have underlying meanings which it is folly to ignore. It is not wise on arrival to challenge established practice and well worn habits such as seating arrangements or any other time honoured rituals. The reasons for what at first may seem eccentricities are bound to emerge eventually, and any reforming zeal could be taken as impertinence or insensitivity. Better to invest thought and effort appreciating the subtleties and intricacies of the power relations of the staffroom in order to become established swiftly and effectively.

Crass behaviour, such as smoking when it clearly gives offence or monopolising the telephone, might seem too obvious to point out but it is surprising how often I hear established staff comment on this sort of behaviour. Interpersonal skills of a high order are expected of teachers, and if these are wanting in a new member of staff the inescapable conclusions will be drawn. Judgements are being made from the outset, and, though these may not appear to have professional relevance, they are part and parcel of 'sizing you up'.

There is an element of socialisation involved as well. The messages may be overt or covert but they will convey the priorities and values which the staff hold dear. Years ago it might have been hard to distinguish at first between staffroom 'rules' on one hand and the dictates of an overbearing grandee on the other. Now things are far more relaxed. If it is difficult sometimes to be patient with trivia, there is usually someone on hand who will provide an explanation or at least see it in the same light as you do. If the staffroom is to be a haven in which its members can relax and be themselves (a particular necessity for a new teacher who might be struggling to present a professional front in the classroom which may be at odds with his or her own self) then there are essential features which must be guarded. Privacy and confidentiality are key factors and everyone has a responsibility to protect them.

Personal privacy

There are several sorts of privacy which must be respected in order for the staffroom to be felt a safe place. Teachers are entitled to be sure that they can be free to talk without their personal lives being the subject of discussion outside the staffroom. This protection is essential when irresponsible talk might cause pupils to be provided with fuel for speculation or gossip. Information such as telephone numbers and addresses which might result in a nuisance or worse must never be made public or needlessly disclosed. It was through such an indiscretion that, as a young teacher, I was put on the mailing list of a catalogue company by a pupil, much to my irritation and embarrassment.

While the ultimate protection lies in the responsibility of the individual to withhold personal information, this is an unrealistic stance to adopt at an interpersonal level when the very nature of functioning as a professional staff demands a level of trust and openness and therefore a degree of self-disclosure and sharing. This does pose a dilemma for a new teacher who naturally wants to become accepted. Try to strike a balance between staying aloof and becoming too involved.

Pupils' privacy is also a matter of professional importance and needs to be respected. Erring on the side of caution is probably the best advice. Any temptation to announce juicy gossip should be resisted on a 'do as you would be done by' basis, if for no loftier reason. Some staffrooms have a 'strictly confidential' board for sensitive information but it must be remembered that this alone is not a guarantee of privacy.

Gossip

A well-guarded tongue is an asset for a new teacher and yet it is a difficult thing to preserve. Newcomers are bound to need to confide in someone yet sometimes feel there is a risk in admitting mistakes and divulging information which puts them in a poor light. Caution is needed here particularly since fatigue and distress can prompt ill-advised disclosure.

It can happen that in the process of getting to know who's who, exaggerated stories can be put about by colleagues which are best taken with a pinch of salt. Passing on gossip can create dire tangles which, in the often intense atmosphere of a staffroom, can be regretted later. It is better to steer clear of these minefields as a matter of personal as well as professional preservation. An essential pre-caution in some staffrooms is the identification of the resident 'mole' with the hot line to the Head. Some Heads do not appear in the staffroom at all and deliberately avoid the staffroom chat while others are more involved. Gaining a reputation for being reserved is a small price to pay for avoiding involvement in gossip. It is best to be thought trustworthy and reliable. Initially the staff can only judge you on limited evidence, but first impressions will be telling. Although professional trust is built over time, new staff need to feel that eventually they will secure sympathy and support.

All this is a matter of personality as well as the way new staff respond to the situation in which they find themselves. There is no substitute for a friendly, open approach, especially if it is reciprocated.

Getting on with colleagues

Professional relationships in the staffroom are important to the extent that good working partnerships can enhance the overall atmosphere as well as motivating staff to cooperate in a positive way. In teaching, as in most occupations, you are as good as you give, and if your colleagues encourage this by welcoming your contribution and valuing your efforts then so much the better. Much of this depends on good leadership and skilful, though not necessarily conspicuous, management on the part of the Head.

Obviously this happy situation cannot be contrived, and however willing people are to work hard as teachers, this may not overcome personal dislike or group dynamics which fall short of the ideal. New teachers may find it difficult to join an existing group, especially if they feel isolated and conspicuous by reason of age and inexperience. In these circumstances the best advice is to concentrate on the areas of work which are entirely within your scope to accomplish, and gradually to gain trust and respect through the quality of your work. On the other hand, beware of an unhappy self-imposed isolation through immersing yourself too deeply in your work.

Professional relationships in the staffroom become more significant in stressful times. Major disruption can occur in a group when any reorganisation poses a threat to status or stability. It might be the amalgamation of subjects, the appointment of a senior manager or threats of redundancy. Teachers are becoming familiar with disturbing events such as these which were unheard of until recent years. No-one is fireproof or immune to the difficulties caused by the need to maintain ordinary day-to-day relationships in the face of change and its consequences.

A new member of staff may well be on the sidelines of these sorts of developments, but nevertheless be caught in the crossfire between overstressed colleagues. It is some comfort to remember that when senior managers are subjected to severe pressure, the tension inevitably gets passed on down the line, perhaps unwittingly.

Awkward relationships

New teachers, in common with all young people launching themselves into the workplace, may run into trouble thanks to over-enthusiastic colleagues who may see them as fair game for teasing or an obvious target for jokes. Personalities are the key to this, of course. It does not need to be said that individuals undertake their own responsibilities in this regard, but people do vary in their ability to cope, and the vulnerability of new staff can be irresistible to those who should know better. The point of drawing attention to these unspecified hazards is that sometimes young teachers are reluctant to take action if they feel uncomfortable about the behaviour of colleagues towards them. Teachers are generally assumed to be good people, and well meaning. Nevertheless there may be situations in the intense and sometimes claustrophobic atmosphere of the staffroom where emotions can run high, and it is as well to realise this. Rather than descending into gloom at this point one can recognize that there are also cheering examples of relationships which blossom in the staffroom. However wholesome, these are best kept from the school gossips inside and outside the staffroom.

Harassment

Anything which amounts to sexual harassment must never be tolerated and should be dealt with sooner rather than later, however painful and embarrassing it is to report. This is a good case for having the protection of a union at an early stage in the hope that you do not later need to have recourse to their legal services.

It is also important to realise that provocation must in no way be given. Headteachers can be put in a difficult position over staff relationships. If private matters are reported to them or a member of staff makes a formal complaint, they must take action. Although they might prefer not to become involved, they are still bound in the last analysis to react over anything which impinges on the welfare of the staff and the children.

Induction

Some of the key relationships which dominate the early years of teaching may be conducted, not so much in the staff room, but rather in the office of the Headteacher or whoever is responsible for probationers. Your induction into teaching will ideally be a carefully prepared programme incorporating opportunities for you to meet other probationers in the same position, offering ready access to help and support as you need it and providing professional extension of your initial training and the means to achieve your career plan.

An induction programme should be seen as the beginning of a continuing process of personal and professional development and not just a contingency plan of coping skills to survive the first year. From the outset the assessment procedures which will be used to guage your progress during the probationary year must be perfectly clear to all those who are involved, the details of criteria, timing, format and individual responsibilities outlined and understood. Linked with this is the absolute necessity to include formative assessment and opportunities for professional guidance.

It would obviously make sense if the kinds of self-appraisal and profiling which were carried out during initial teacher training could be continued into your first post; in the absence of nationwide induction criteria this is unrealistic at present. Using material contained in an existing profile would provide useful information to the school, enabling appropriate help to be given.

Contact with other probationers can be very helpful either 'in house' in a large school or as part of a borough-wide scheme. A teacher I know derived great benefit and pleasure from a series of lunch-time sessions to which the probationers in her school were invited. They were run by a deputy head and took the form of a purposeful, practical introduction to a range of topics relevant to new staff. Although the formal induction of new staff is recognised as an important responsibility which is undertaken by the school, informally the new teacher will be inducted by all members of staff who are able to contribute to this process.

All being well, the structure of your induction will be in place and you will have an opportunity to negotiate with the member of staff responsible for probationers in order that the particular needs and interests which you have identified can be included.

Asking for help

If little in the way of induction seems to be materialising, check with friends in other schools to compare notes. Consider what you feel you need and, once enough time has elapsed for the dust to settle at the beginning of term, begin to enquire in the right quarters what induction plans are in store for your probationary year.

The difficulty of this is not to be underestimated. You may feel reluctant to seem demanding when surrounded by what, in the hectic life of a school, may seem more urgent priorities than your personal concerns. Just remember two important things. Firstly, in the general school hurly-burly, the plight of a newcomer is easily overlooked. This is no reflection of how you are regarded so don't respond by shrinking away. Secondly, it is patently in the interest of the school to ensure that you embark on your teaching career with the best support that can be provided, and it therefore benefits the school to provide effective means of induction. The squeaky wheel gets the oil, so insist on getting the attention you need and are entitled to expect.

The way in which you are seen to take responsibility for your own progress in teaching will contribute to the impression you make on the staff as a whole and particularly on those whose responsibility it is to oversee your professional development.

It would be naïve to suppose that, even in a large school, the Head is too remote to monitor the activities and progress of new staff. There is an important aspect of the relationship between the Headteacher and new staff to consider and that is the direction of their teaching time. The impact of 'directed time' impinges more on the margins of professional activity than on a teacher's day-to-day timetable. This applies to all teachers and not just probationers. However it is recognised that a lighter timetable in the first year can make an enormous difference to a teacher's ability to cope and allowance should be made for this.

'Directed time' it must be stressed, is the responsibility of the Head who arranges that each member of staff works for 1265 hours in the course of the working year and that the timetable which implements the school curriculum is taught. On the margins of regular teaching duties, directed time is the mechanism whereby extra-curricular activities can be organised and the involvement of the staff and their dedication is recognised. While there have been problems with this approach to the management of staff time, it does have the merit for new staff, of clarifying the boundaries of their work commitment.

Assessment of the probationer

When you meet the member of staff who will be responsible for you as a probationary teacher you should clarify as a matter of urgency exactly what your responsibilities are and exactly what expectations she or he will have of you. You also need to have a clear idea of how the relationship will work out in practice so that you know to what extent you will be required to consult other teachers and to review and analyse your progress. Do not hesitate to ask how your progress will be assessed and whether you will be actively involved in the appraisal process. You need to know whether you can expect to receive a copy of the reports made on you and also to know to whom the reports are sent.

It is true that you may sometimes experience a gap between the promise and the reality but the point is to establish communication and as close an understanding as possible. I have heard exasperated, well-meaning staff in charge of probationers complain that they cannot sense any trust between themselves and their young colleagues who seem impervious to their offers of help or advice. While on a personal level this might be understandable, professionally, you would be foolish to resist the help which is available. At the other extreme, some new staff exhibit such dependency that their mentors despair: but at least this is easier to tackle than the isolating effects of denying that anything is wrong. The last thing you want to happen in your probationary year is to alienate the very person who will be writing your reports and commenting on your suitability as a teacher. A new teacher badly needing to succeed and confirm the promise of his or her training, looks constantly for answers and reassurance. It is essential for this to be provided by someone whose judgement is trusted and who can be relied upon to convey approval or criticism with skill and understanding.

If there is a serious clash of personality with a key member of staff who will significantly influence your early progress in teaching you are stuck with a major problem. Good judgement is needed to assess whether the situation is just mildly disappointing but not worth making a fuss about or whether it is severe enough to warrant taking some action and risking the consequences in the hope of something more satisfactory being established. You need to consider who to approach for help. My advice would be to go to the Head in the first instance and only if this proves unsatisfactory to consult the LEA advisor who is responsible for probationers. Other courses of action include complaining to fellow sufferers; remembering of course that they will not be able to provide practical solutions, and seeking help from your union while bearing in mind that such a step would increase the gravity of the situation considerably.

Your contact with the headteacher

Your contact with the Head will depend on such factors as the size of your school and its geography as much as the way a personal relationship works out. You may encounter the Head frequently or (especially in a large secondary school) hardly at all. Much will depend on his or her management style and the organisation of the school.

When it comes to professional assessment and the report at the end of the probationary year, I always tell my students the tale of the probationer who was dismayed by the lukewarm report he received at the end of what had been a very successful first year of teaching. He pointed out to the Head that in the categories of attendance and punctuality he thought he deserved a better verdict than 'fair' because he had never actually been either late or absent. The revised version which appeared the next day not only showed 'excellent' instead of 'fair', but the rest of the report had been revised in the same vein and came nearer to acknowledging the good work which had been done. I mention this not to ridicule the Head's judgement but to present an example of a brave and appropriately assertive approach by a young teacher, a case of fortune favouring the bold. It is also an example of a young teacher exercising his own professional judgement and the essential skill of self-evaluation. Good work rarely goes unnoticed even within the almost private setting of a quiet classroom but new teachers cannot enjoy the luxury of an established reputation, they can only work towards it.

On the whole, conditions for probationers are more favourable now than they used to be. It is realised that they are a precious resource, especially in times of teacher shortage, and they therefore must be cherished. This at any rate is the intention. I think that teachers in the main, being caring types, have always helped young staff to find their feet; the difference now is that it is official and backed to some extent with resources such as timetable release and specific guidance as well as deliberate induction arrangements and opportunities for professional mentoring.

CHAPTER 5

Teachers and Parents

In my experience both as a parent and as a teacher, the more frequent and positive the contacts between home and school, the more mutual reassurance can be generated to the child's ultimate benefit.

It is asking a great deal of teachers to go out of their way to meet parents either socially or in a more formal capacity, since the demands made on them in the course of a normal working day are already heavy. The importance of communications between teachers and parents is underlined by the provision which is now available to Heads in directing the time of staff, so that attendance at Parents' Evenings is part of their contract. In addition to this, most teachers are more than generous with their time and value highly the benefits which can come from a good relationships with parents. It is particularly gratifying as a teacher to be able to strike up a relationship with other adults whose cooperation can make the task of teaching more satisfactory and often positively more successful. Nevertheless encounters with parents can be among the most daunting experiences in store for new teachers.

Inexperienced staff may feel that, while they manage to present a convincingly confident front to the pupils, perhaps even to colleagues, they may find it hard to maintain this professional stance with parents. Parents can seem to have an impressive authority both by reason of their greater age and experience and their parental expertise. New teachers may be loath to challenge parents who are naturally and rightly disposed to defend their young. Even if they agree with an unfavourable judgement on their offspring, parents with feelings of loyalty will only be able to take so much criticism of their children and it is well to be aware of this. The best approach to take is to be honest without being aggressive. The word 'partnership' is often used to describe the ideal relationship between home, school and the other stakeholders in the education system. In order to mean anything, this needs to take the form of parents getting actively involved in the education process in which parents and teachers are prepared to learn from listening to each other.

Primary teachers are less likely to feel distant from parents than secondary staff through frequent informal contact and the relative simplicity of exchanging messages, particularly when children are taken to and from school. During the early years of schooling there are numerous opportunities for casual meetings which reinforce communications and strengthen relationships.

Secondary pupils tend to put some distance between home and school through their increasing independence and while, in theory, they should be more dependable in passing on messages, they are more than capable too of sabotage and distortion. Parents' Evenings are a formal opportunity to establish face-to-face contact with parents and here there is great potential for the disposal of unreal images and myths which may otherwise create tension on both sides. It is idle to suggest to a young teacher that there is nothing to fear from the visitation of a succession of unknown adults, often in pairs, whose main aim is assumed to be to support their offspring come what may, challenge teaching methods and lesson content and demand reports and predictions of examination results. Equally, the comments from some parents can be a source of assurance for the new teacher. Although Parents' Evenings can be very taxing both mentally and emotionally, in my experience they were extremely useful and rewarding.

Preparing for Parents' Evening

Obviously any previous encounters you may have had can help to lessen any nervousness but there are several practical steps to take whether or not you have met parents beforehand.

First of all, you are there to discuss your pupils' progress and will therefore be expected to have all the relevant information at your fingertips. It is useful to be armed with your register and markbook as well as duplicates of reports if they were issued prior to the meeting. You are at a distinct disadvantage if parents have in front of them remarks which you wrote some time ago and you have nothing to remind you of what you said. If it isn't too cumbersome, sets of books or recent examples of homework can be helpful to illustrate your comments, whether critical or complimentary, and to establish some common understanding.

When discussing children's work, progress and behaviour, try to avoid jargon and be wary of making assumptions of mutual understanding which are not warranted. Clarity and simplicity are preferable even when you feel the need of a verbal smoke screen in an emergency.

Secondary schools increasingly encourage pupils to be present at discussions between parents and teachers, and this has many advantages. Pupils are able to gauge the concern for them which is demonstrated by these meetings. There is a reduced likelihood of the misinterpretation or bias that can creep into the reporting of the discussions when they take place between teachers and parents alone. Apart from any other considerations, in a busy demanding evening, at least in the presence of the pupil, there is no danger of having the wrong one in mind when you are talking. Nevertheless a new teacher in a secondary school may well be in the difficult position of meeting parents to discuss a pupil he or she hardly knows. In a well organised school this should be anticipated, perhaps by arranging for new staff to sit with their head of department.

It may be helpful for new teachers to consider what sort of experience parents may be anticipating from a formal Parents' Evening. Nervousness and anxiety can beset the most poised and apparently successful parent. There is so much at stake at every stage in their child's development and though parents may appear to be demanding and in a position to make judgements, they also frequently feel that their competence as a parent is being judged. Particularly vulnerable are mothers who go out to work, single parents, parents who are much older or much younger than the others and parents who do not feel particularly successful themselves, as well as parents of children who, for one reason or another are not making progress or are badly behaved at school. Parents who are teachers themselves have the potential to be both extremely understanding and sympathetic or, at the other extreme, canny and pushy (especially when it comes to predicted exam grades and entry to Higher Education).

Teachers are used to keeping records of their pupils' academic progress, but they are not necessarily expected to be as thorough when it comes to the pastoral aspects of their work where professional judgement might be just as important. Accounting to parents should refer to the whole child and this means all school activities, not only academic work. As a form tutor you may be just as concerned about absences, instances of bullying or referral from other staff, and in order to present a case to parents it helps to have facts at hand rather than rely on what may appear to be anecdotal evidence. This is particularly important if the parents refuse to acknowledge information about their child which may be distasteful or painful.

Arrangements for contacting parents

Teachers are not necessarily able to contact (or avoid) parents, as they please. In practice, these relationships are subject to certain constraints. There are established practices by which schools operate, monitor and regulate the contact which the school has with parents both formally and informally. On a practical level, the size of the school will dictate these matters as will the management style which influences the organisation of the school. Even in the most free and easy atmosphere, there has to be a system whereby important information from parents is conveyed to the relevant people on the staff.

Some schools allow initiative in contacting parents to be taken by the class teacher provided a record is kept and important information is passed on. Safeguards for both parents and teachers must be provided when it comes to privacy and the possible encroachment into personal time and territory on either side.

Teaching does attract people with a concern for the welfare of others, and an enthusiastic new teacher may need to have boundaries placed on this aspect of his or her role. Situations can often arise where concern for a pupil extends to the family, and inappropriate, though well meant, involvements can result which are difficult to shed. When dealing with parents, new teachers need to follow the example of colleagues and be guided by their local knowledge and experience. Your own instinct and judgement need not be suspended, however. You may, for example, react against staffroom labelling of families which may strike you as unfair or against the interests of your pupil. Keep colleagues in the picture about anything which you uncover unless a private matter arises which could be an issue of confidentiality or potentially a subject for gossip.

Interviewing parents

More serious discussions with parents are usually conducted in private, and it is reasonable to involve senior staff in arranging for this to happen even if you conduct the interview yourself. Sometimes, though, an innocuous conversation takes a serious turn and it can be quite unnerving for a new teacher to be confronted by extremes of emotion, distressing disclosures and even downright hostility, all of which can be personally intimidating. Obviously you must avoid unseemly arguments, but it is not easy to face excessively demanding parents and you may need the help of more experienced colleagues.

This is far from suggesting that new teachers are the natural prey of hordes of parents who make unreasonable demands. Nonetheless, lack of confidence and experience can result in tricky moments when a senior colleague, if present, could come to the rescue if necessary.

Written contact with parents

Written correspondence with parents can be easier to cope with because it can be more considered, though I still smart at the recollection of the response I had from an indignant father whose daughter's behaviour I had described, in a restrained understatement, as 'giddy'. Always keep a copy of letters you send to parents along with their replies. They may need to be retained in the child's file when the correspondence is complete. Explanations of absence must always be kept carefully and noted in the register. Forged notes are not unknown and since a new teacher is more likely to be presented with a fake, it is a wise precaution to take more than a passing interest in the authenticity of notes.

Phoning home

Telephone communications between parents and teachers are more frequent now as any harassed school secretary will testify. Teachers are wise if they make and keep notes of any calls and their content. The temptation to contact parents by ringing from your own home should be avoided even though it may be the only opportunity you have to make these calls. Apart from your increased phone bill, you need to make a firm distinction, as clear to yourself as to the parents, between home and school in order to protect your personal time. If necessary, press for more sensible access to the school phone lines or more time to contact parents in school hours.

Primary teachers are more likely to be able to contact parents in school hours if they are at home with other young children. If you need to follow up a suspected truant from secondary school you are quite likely to get them of of bed so only bother if it is to remind them of a public examination that day which they are about to miss. Protect your home telephone number from parents and if there is a danger of being troubled at home, consider going ex-directory as a further safeguard.

Home visits

Visiting pupils' homes is less usual for secondary school staff than primary. Most local authorities employ home/school liaison staff which takes care of what in some circumstances can be a difficult task. In addition, Education Social Workers (some are still known as Education Welfare Officers – EWOs) visit families as part of their work, typically to investigate regular absence from school. My own experience has shown me that calling at a pupil's home will not necessarily remove the frustration and anxiety felt by a teacher worried by a pupil's persistant, unexplained non-attendance. The potential for embarrassment on both sides is considerable and for most teachers it is not regarded as part of their job. Such a step should not be undertaken without the knowledge and agreement of the Head and a full report should always be given.

On the other hand, some aspects of home visiting can be extremely constructive, as when teachers visit the homes of young children about to start school. Some home-school reading projects in the primary schools also include home-visiting to support parents and offer guidance. The value of home-visiting varies therefore according to circumstances, and its chances of success are usually greater if they are part of a coherent school policy concerning, for example, transition to junior school or a scheme to involve parents in some aspect of the curriculum.

Parents' access

An increasingly frequent concern of teachers is the need to know which children are the subject of court orders when this means that one or other parent is denied access to their child. An obvious opportunity for a deprived parent to make contact is as the child leaves school and the school may be expected to cooperate in preventing a parent from having access in this way. In such a case all staff will probably be informed while some may be more personally involved. On the other hand, when care and custody is shared, both parents may have to be contacted when information is sent to parents, where in the normal run of things, the message simply goes to the child's home to either one or both parents.

Complications can set in when parents remarry, change their names, adopt children, move house, split up and so on. While all of this is dealt with by the school administration once the school is officially informed, there can be hiccups at an informal level. Children can pass on family details which turn out not to be accurate. The task of verifying what they say can be delicate, to put it mildly. New staff need to be aware of these matters even though they might not be directly concerned.

Parents in school

Parents by and large are welcome in schools and they may be present in a variety of roles. When they actually work at the school this will soon be apparent. When they are involved as 'adults other than teachers' (AOTs) their role is likely to be well defined and made clear by the management. New teachers will quickly see how to use the valuable contribution they can make.

Parents can be present in the classroom giving voluntary assistance in dozens of ways, either on a regular basis or by putting in the occasional guest appearance. New teachers would be advised to consult experienced colleagues in order to manage these valuable resources effectively.

Less predictable and harder to handle are the parents who visit the school without an appointment and who need time to talk, though this may be less of a problem in a primary school. The organisation of the school may lend itself to unannounced visits but even when it is really not convenient, a parent who is upset may not fully appreciate the situation, or the fact that other priorities exist for the teacher and the class. When this happens, there is probably an arrangement whereby the parent is invited to wait until the next break and a message is sent to alert the teacher concerned. By its very nature, an unannounced visit is likely to be urgent and simply offering an appointment at another time is unlikely to be an adequate response. If a conversation takes longer than the free time you have available, call on senior staff to take your class or to continue the interview. It is always wise to make it clear from the outset how much time you have to talk and stick to what you say. Always offer to arrange a meeting at a more convenient time if the matter would otherwise be left unresolved.

Parents and governors

Apart from individual school initiatives, there have been efforts through legislation in recent years to involve parents far more in the education of their children. Indeed this aim is a main feature underlying some of the provisions of the Education Reform Act 1988 and the Education Act 1986. Parental involvement at an official level has been attempted in a number of ways. The reform of the Governing bodies of schools represents an attempt to widen community involvement and to change the balance of power wielded by the groups represented.

The governing body of each school has at least two parent governors who are elected by the parent body. This is not an easy position to fill, since a mandate from such an amorphous group is well nigh impossible. In practice parent governors are there in a personal capacity to contribute their common sense and sound judgement for the benefit of the school.

By law, since the Education Act of 1986, each school is obliged to hold an annual meeting for parents and governors. Staff are usually notified of this meeting and are welcome to attend, but in practice you would only be required to be present if there was a particular issue at stake which directly affected your work. So far the general impression is that these meetings have been disappointingly attended with many of them being inquorate (20% of parents are needed for formal motions to be proposed) and many where the governors have outnumbered the parents. The claim made by some LEAs that this indicates that parents must be satisfied with the status quo is hardly convincing. The purpose of greater involvement at this level is clearly not yet being achieved, but perhaps these are early days.

This annual meeting with the governors has to be preceded by the publication and distribution of an annual report to parents. This will include a wide range of essential, detailed information about the school and an update of the current school documents such as the school prospectus, an outline of the complaints procedure, information about the curriculum and details of teaching programmes.

Parents Associations

If there is a Parents Association at your school, you may be expected to join in some of the activities which it organises. In the main, these associations are groups of parents who form a committee with the aim of supporting the school in fundraising activities and providing social occasions for the families of the children. Money raising is far more vital now considering the resource implications of Local Management of Schools. Your enthusiasm for these events will probably depend on the state of your social life, your affinity with the parent age group or your interest in the activities on offer.

Parent-Teacher associations

Parent-Teacher Associations tend to be more formal than Parents Associations and are more of a forum for discussion. At one time Heads were inclined to be wary of such groups but in the present climate they can provide support and feedback and can be a positive asset. Although newcomers are likely to be welcomed with open arms, it tends to be long-established staff who offer their services to the PTA since they tend to know the parents involved. The likelihood is that the impact of the LMS legislation may provoke more active interest from parents in school concerns since decision-making is now much more in the hands of individual schools. In fact, financial constraints may succeed in eliciting involvement where many of the ploys such as exhibitions and shows have failed to attract interest. If parents feel that they have more control over decision-making, and if they are going to be asked to finance their children's education in ways which had previously not been necessary, it may produce some keen interest in the way that activities are funded. It does produce for Heads the interesting problem which arises when 'he who pays the piper calls the tune'. It is difficult when a group of parents raise money for a pet project, a new school mini-bus for example, if the Head is desperate for the money to improve the plumbing in the loos and yet cannot afford to look a gift horse in the mouth. It must be a sign of the times that swimming pools are no longer mentioned by even the most ardent fundraiser. Glamour is definitely out.

Parents and the curriculum

Since the Education Reform Act and the changes in the examinations at 16+, parents have had many more chances to find out what is happening in schools and opportunities in some cases to influence events. Not all parents, however, take advantage of these opportunities. Some parents are concerned about general education policy in a community context or from a political stance, while others are only interested where their own children are directly affected. Again, many parents, having satisfied themselves that the schools they have chosen for their children are efficient and will carry out the promise of their prospectus, are happy to let professionals get on with their job. However, there is ample research evidence to show that a pupil's achievement is improved considerably when parents and teachers cooperate by taking a joint close interest in both homework and school work.

Ideally, teachers welcome a level of involvement which is based on genuine interest and cooperation, somewhere between those who let sleeping dogs lie until a crisis erupts and those who take an obsessive interest in the minutiae of their children's education. A recent report by education inspectors warns that parental involvement in schools can waste teacher's time unless activities are carefully planned. They commented on the 'fine line between help and hindrance' though they also commented on the benefits which an effective home-school partnership can bring.

A good Head will set a positive tone in your school where contacts with parents are concerned. New staff, if they are wise, will follow this lead and use every opportunity to foster contacts and give parents as much access to what is going on in the classroom as is compatible with teaching their children effectively.

Reports to parents

Communicating with parents via written reports is a traditional feature of British education. School reports have always been taken very seriously by parents but sometimes as a bit of a joke by everyone else. The DES now require annual reports for all children to be sent to parents. Under the regulations which came into force in August 1990, school reports must include information on progress in all the National Curriculum subjects as they are phased in, as well as reference to other activities such as work experience or community service. Although the statutory compulsion refers to annual reports (to be completed by the end of July except in the case of pupils who are over 16, when they need only to be ready for the end of September), schools are to regard these as the legal minimum and to report more frequently if necessary.

The government has decided that a common format would make for a more standardised, coherent report which will be especially helpful for employers. Although the regulations specify in some detail the information which parents are entitled to know, they do not stipulate that they take the form of written comments as distinct from statistical information such as progress towards National Curriculum targets. Most schools, though, will include written remarks to amplify the bald assessment scores. This is likely to be a matter decided in the context of the overall school policy on assessment, recording and reporting and new staff should acquaint themselves with this. As a result of these changes, reports will inevitably be regarded in a different light by both teachers and parents, and should facilitate a more constructive dialogue.

Access to files

Parents now have access to their children's files, and statutory regulations require them to be accurate and up-to-date. Parental access to these records is allowed by the Education (School Records) Regulations 1989 and applies to pupils under 18. Those over 18 are able to see their own records. Records held on computer are subject to the Data Protection Act 1984 which ensures open access to the information. While no-one would mourn the passing of the 'Makes no trouble and takes none' variety of one-liner reports, the emerging picture is not without its problems. You should take your cue from the Head or your head of department when it comes to report writing. Individuality should not be suppressed, but there is likely to be a 'house style' to which you are expected to conform. Remember that what you write in reports has a wider audience than the parents only. Your comments will be read by your head of department if you have one, other staff in the process of collating the reports as well as whoever is designated to censor and check for errors.

Your first sets of reports will probably be monitored until confidence is established in your work. It is a good idea to ask to see examples of well written reports before you embark on your first set. If you write thoughtful, positive, encouraging and fluent remarks, they will say as much about you as they say about the children. It will save a great deal of trouble in the long run if you write your reports with a dictionary at your elbow. Have your register and mark book to hand so that you write with authority on the evidence before you. Reports which are vague and bland are a lost opportunity to send a useful message home so make sure that those which you send are positive and helpful.

Records of achievement

An additional recent development is the increasing interest in Records of Achievement. You may well have encountered teachers working with pupils on their Record of Achievement and you will understand that this is an initiative which has been the subject of several pilot schemes around the country. One of the aims has been to devise a method whereby all pupils' achievements are included in a final summary giving evidence of their work and of any accomplishments which give them credit. The pilot schemes also emphasised the formative aspects of appreciating and recording achievement.

Part of the process depends on personal and work-related guidance interviews which are arranged for pupils with their tutors and include the negotiation of action plans and personal targets. In other words, standards are raised by involving pupils in decision-making about their own learning. Preparing these records is notoriously time consuming although the pupils benefit enormously through the scope for individual attention which the scheme allows.

It is now Government policy that some of the key principles of ROAs will be incorporated into the National Curriculum in order to provide a précis of evidence of achievement that has hitherto been provided by traditional school reports. The DES has laid down minimum summative requirements for ROAs, but schools can add to these to emphasise the aspects which engage pupils' personal involvement.

Whatever pattern is adopted for reporting purposes, you must not lose track of the fact that ROAs are one of several means of communicating with parents, and that the overall aim is that pupils should benefit from the interchange of information and the shared concern of all those involved.

Pupils' records

Pupil records are in future to be subject to strict regulation. A file must be kept for each pupil, and there will be careful arrangements in schools for operating the system. It may be that your school only records grades rather than comments, for example, to indicate academic progress. There will be strict guidelines which govern what is included on the pupils' record in your school and you will be informed exactly how the system is to work.

It is unlikely that you will be in a position to agonise about what should be retained in the files of individual pupils, but you will be responsible for the information which you enter. You must take as much care with this as you would with spoken comments and remember that parents have now been given access to these records. As for any records kept on computer, the Data Protection Act 1984 entitles anyone to obtain a copy of personal information about themselves held electronically.

It should go without saying that the information held in files, whether manual or on disc must be accurate and kept up-to-date. Generally the more access there is to files, the less they reveal. If there is an atmosphere of cooperation between parents and teachers the potential for paranoia over reports and files will be minimal as will the scope for inaccurate or prejudiced remarks.

When you write material which will be included in pupils' records, you need to bear in mind the audience. Your style may vary, though the format is likely to be governed by the regulations which apply. Teachers sometimes include items of information, warnings, comments, correspondence and so on in children's files, and then remove them later if circumstances change or if they are no longer relevant or true. Even where it is well-intentioned, it is unlikely that there will be much scope for idiosyncratic record keeping once the new regulations are well established.

Teachers may be inclined to keep their own records on pupils privately in which case they will be confidential unless passed on to another member of staff. Although private records may be useful for individual members of staff, somehow it seems a contradiction when the general trend is towards operating a more open system.

Finally, while every effort is made to involve parents in all aspects of school life this should not simply be a matter of pious intent but one of deliberate effort. Some schools achieve an enthusiastic response from parents which makes a real difference to the school. Active parents can sit on school committees, offer professional services, and contribute to the social life of the school but anyone can become an effective 'partner' in their child's education by communicating, supporting, and fostering positive and enthusiastic attitudes and this is more likely to happen if parents feel that their efforts are valued by the school.

CHAPTER 6

Out of School

'Out of school' would seem to be a self-explanatory term. As it happens, however, there needs to be a clear understanding of the different practical applications of the expression. Obviously it includes 'off-site' activities which are part of the school curriculum, such as games lessons and school journeys. Usually these activities take place within school hours as a matter of day-to-day routine, even though they may require parental permission as well as the levy of a charge or perhaps extra supervision by staff before they can take place.

Before and after school

Less obviously 'out of school' can also include the time before and after school where children are present and provision must be made for them. Each school will make arrangements according to need, and staff cooperation will be expected – or even 'directed' – usually on a rota basis. The arrangements or lack of them will be made known to parents as a matter of course. Some 'out of school' activities involve a considerable change of routine and a great deal of careful organisation, little of which will fall to the lot of probationary teachers since, for the purposes of most of the LEA regulations which apply, they are not likely to be included in the definition of 'teacher'.

Outings

The prospect of an outing or indeed any break from school routine is often welcomed by the staff as much as it is by the pupils. I rate it highly as one of the best ways of whipping up enthusiasm and creating an opportunity for enjoyment in lessons.

When GCSE was first mooted, in the early eighties, a frequently proclaimed advantage was that the new examination would enable pupils to venture outside school in order to explore, investigate, draw on the local environment for stimulus and generally broaden their educational experiences. Ironically, there have since been counter-vailing forces at work which have been making 'out of school' out of the question in a way which many teachers regret. These are the introduction of 'directed time', the problems with charging and the importance of conforming to the stringent regulations which now apply to out of school activities.

Directed time

Directed time means that each teacher is contracted to work for 1265 hours a year spread over 195 days. The Head determines how that time is spent and, outside these hours, it is up to the professional judgement of the individual teacher to choose how much time to devote to school work. This inevitably means that directed time for extra-curricular activities is limited. Equally inevitably, teachers' attitudes are affected by being directed in an area which had previously secured their generous commitment. The danger now is that the enthusiasm of particular members of staff for outside activities will not find an outlet and that pupils and staff will be deprived of the opportunities which used to exist.

Charging

The stipulation that 'out of school' activities must not, except under certain specified conditions, incur a charge, puts a constraint on what a school can provide for its pupils.

The situation arose from the perfectly reasonable premise that education should be free and therefore charging was outlawed. As a result, many activities which hitherto had been organised by schools and to which parents contributed had to be discontinued if school budgets could not cover the cost. Each school will have its own ways of dealing with these difficulties and new staff will be shown how they operate.

Accidents

The fact that there have been some tragic accidents on school trips in recent years has given rise to serious investigations and detailed reports resulting in much stricter LEA guidelines to govern these activities. In fact the guidelines are now so thorough that organising a trip presents a daunting prospect, enough to deter the most confident and experienced teacher. The local education authority carries overall responsibility for official 'out of school' activities and they all provide guidance which must be followed scrupulously.

In spite of these warnings, no new teacher should be put off the idea of accompanying colleagues on a school trip, in fact this is just the time to join in so that you can observe what is involved and enjoy the experience without being burdened with any responsibility other than the usual teacher's duty of being *in loco parentis*.

Some teachers organise trips down to the last detail and take great pride in the achievement of monumental feats such as removing whole year groups for a couple of weeks; in the process they earn the gratitude of the rest of the school as well as of the parents. A star performer in this department was the Head of the school where my mother taught who used to provide sherry from a thermos flask for the staff on school journeys. She would never get away with dispensing this 'medicine' in these safety-conscious times. It was a demure little treat too, unlikely to bring the profession into disrepute in the way recently reported of some teachers in charge of school parties on cross-Channel ferries. Some people have a talent for organising trips successfully. It is something special to be able to do for children and you will find, if you are interested and take the trouble to offer your services, just how rewarding it can be.

Probationers and outings

Even as a probationer and bearing in mind that you may not be covered to take on the responsibility of organising visits, you need to be familiar with the LEA guidelines which apply to your school or govern particular activities, such as the number of staff required. A young teacher I knew was unhappy at having sole charge of a group of lively fifteen year olds she was taking on a visit. She rightly complained to the Head, having been supported by indignant colleagues and I was duly sent along as a back-up, leaving my class to their own devices. There was no question of what should take priority once the matter had been raised.

Young teachers are expected to have the energy and enthusiasm needed to engage in out-of-school activities. They may have more flexible lives and be more available to undertake this work than older staff who may be more tied by family responsibilities. Nevertheless, probationers should not be taken for granted. Once involved, if you find that you are doing most of the hard work of the organisation, just to do it with good grace and put it down to experience. There is much to learn: for example, supply cover for field trips and outings will be part of the cost unless you are covered by a colleague on an informal, reciprocal basis, so this has to be taken into account when planning a jaunt.

I shrink from the task of collecting the pupils' money. My particular vision of Hell is losing any of it. I am not alone in experiencing the panic which can be witnessed in staffrooms throughout the country when cheques go missing and receipts disappear. My worst panic over a visit was when I booked coaches for hundreds of eleven-year-olds for the 24th July instead of the 24th June. I learned the lesson that not only is it necessary to check, but also to get someone to double check for you.

Regulations

Serious emergencies can arise on trips even when thorough arrangements are made and every eventuality seems to have been covered. Procedures to be followed in a crisis are incorporated into the now far more stringent regulations which local authorities issue and which govern all cases of 'Off-Site' and 'Hazardous Activities'. Aware of how peoples' reactions can be unpredictable in an emergency, some authorities issue instructions on durable plastic cards which leaders of parties must carry. Clearly, the larger the enterprise, the more thorough must be the preparation and planning.

The mundane, practical advice which one would pass on to new teachers is in a different league. The administration can be a headache, but you should keep all the documents, permission slips, copies of bills, receipts and so on until well after the event. If the outing was successful and likely to be repeated, then it is useful to have a file with all the relevant information stored and then you will not need to start from scratch the next time.

Always, after any sort of occasion which you have had to organise, make a note of how it went, what was successful about it and what, if the occasion were to be repeated the next day, you would do differently. The easiest approach if you have to organise an out-of-school activity is to rely in the first instance on the usual school routines on these occasions. Each school has its own procedures about collecting and banking money but what you also need to be sure of is that you never to allow a child to give you money unless it is in a sealed envelope with their name and form, the date, the amount, parent's signature on a permission slip and any other vital information.

Residential school trips vary in the supervision required and LEA guidelines are the best indication of procedure. It is important for example that the sleeping arrangements are clear, especially with mixed groups, and also that the ratio of male to female staff roughly matches the ratio of boys to girls.

When it comes to out-of-school activities, schools have their own conventions about dress codes, behaviour in the coach, reporting back and so on, all of which should be made perfectly clear to the pupils before you go. You might as well get all the rules established beforehand to minimise the nagging en route.

It is important for teachers to be consistent and reasonable with pupils and, when you are out with them, forget about relaxing and enjoying the experience. You need to be twice as vigilant and firm as usual. All will then be well and your enjoyment will be the feeling of relief and retrospective pleasure, once you are all back safe and sound.

When you go out, the only thing you cannot really insist on is that someone will think it worth thanking you. I remember feeling quite crestfallen when having brought back safely a group of sixth form boys and girls from a language trip abroad, none of the parents meeting the coach said 'thank you'. As a result I am sure that my expressions of gratitude when my own children go on trips are completely 'over the top', but I do understand the efforts which are made by the staff and what heavy responsibilities they carry when they take children away on school journeys.

After school activities

After school activities can provide you, as a new member of staff, with an chance to make contact with pupils you do not usually teach.

As a rule it is an opportunity to show the extent of your enthusiasm and expertise. This may be a chance to develop a personal interest in an aspect of your subject which the normal curriculum cannot accommodate or it may be, especially in sports and in practical subjects, a chance for you to use equipment and facilities not normally available either to you or to the pupils involved. It would be disingenuous to suggest that teachers run after school activities only out of the goodness of their hearts, but it may be quite a feat of endurance to face the prospect of extending a day which is already tiring, so all credit to those who do so. Extra-curricular activities may give an opportunity for pupils you do not normally teach or who do not have access to your particular area of the curriculum to experience something new. It is certainly a way of meeting pupils on a different basis, and they see you perhaps in a more relaxed frame of mind than usual. You see pupils in a different light too, able to demonstrate their enthusiasm, uninhibited by the usual constraints of the classroom. They are often intrigued by the insight they get into staff interaction, and you need to be aware of this.

At the risk of being a wet blanket, I would caution new staff not to let their hair down too readily under these circumstances. Even though the context is different, the professional relationship of teacher and pupil continues and should not be jeopardised by anything you say or do or allow the pupils to say or do. You will soon recognise when pupils are 'taking advantage' and, though they too may be aware of this, it is your job to draw the line. It is just as important to make sure that children who are involved in after school activities are as safe as they are within school hours.

Permission must be obtained from the head and the governors for any of these activities, and, depending on the ages of the children, permission must also be obtained from their parents. The activities may involve arrangements with the school keeper or changes in travel arrangements, all of which will need to be justified and carefully organised.

You would be wise when planning any activity to prepare a really detailed plan showing exactly what you intend to do. My advice too would be to outline your educational objectives, because schools are all about accountability these days. If you are in a situation where extra-curricular activities are well established and part of the school routine then you may not need to go to these lengths but a newcomer cannot automatically expect to enjoy the same degree of confidence as an established teacher and you might need to justify any new ventures. You will obviously discuss with the Head whether this can be counted as 'directed time'. The initiative may even have come from the Head who, for instance, may propose a school Christmas production.

You might inherit the responsibility for a successful activity from the teacher you replaced and there might be a strong expectation that you will allow it to continue. You may embark on what to you seems a programme of activity with irresistible appeal, only to be disappointed when the children who began with boundless enthusiasm do not have the stamina to match. This may be no reflection on your personal charisma; it may just be that you are not equipped to compete with a favourite television programme or that parents are not happy for children to be travelling home in the dark as the evenings draw in.

It is equally possible that you missed the target when you launched your plans and that you would find more interest in a different age group or by making it plain that both boys and girls would be catered for equally. Some elementary market research would not come amiss and might prevent a false start. Alternatively, rather than launching out on your own, try and team up with a colleague so that you learn the ropes less painfully. You might discover a parent who shares your enthusiasm for flying kites, go-karting, cooking or whatever activity you want to develop. Another adult makes it more fun and provides back-up if you ever have to miss a session and do not want to disappoint the pupils.

Beyond the school gate

Teachers' professional responsibilities may not seem to extend beyond the school gates in most circumstances, apart from when visits and school journeys are arranged.

The exact point at which the school takes over the parents' responsibility is difficult to pinpoint, though it may be a crucial matter, a legal one even, revolving around the duty of care. Primary schools tend to have more closely supervised arrangements than secondary schools but even in secondary schools the essential duty of care exists. What may be difficult to establish should it ever come to a crisis, is the extent of that duty of care and exactly when it ceases. It has to be acknowledged that pupils vary in their personal competence and ability look after themselves. Differing home circumstances too will mean that pupils have varying degrees of independence and this is something which is outside the teacher's influence even though in some circumstances it may seem as though individual parents are imposing too great a responsibility on the school.

Travelling to and from school

While teachers may be aware of how pupils travel to and from school, it is not their business directly. If you are new to the neighbourhood, you gradually get to know from the addresses in the register and from the picture built up by the excuses for lateness, approximately where the children live and how they get to school. It can be useful to learn who lives near whom and which friends travel together.

Impecunious new teachers more than any others are conscious of the state of public transport and consequently of the conditions for pupils' travel if they share the same facilities. What sympathy this might arouse for pupils, however, may well be tempered, if not obliterated, by the unwanted onus of responsibility for reprimanding pupils for any bad behaviour which takes place when they are travelling to and from school. Supervision of bus queues is a duty which needs to be clearly understood and will be a well defined responsibility directed by the Head. It means that you have to exercise a duty of care (as if you were a reasonable parent) just as you do when you are in school. Simply being there indicates the acceptance of responsibility even though there are potentially more dangers – traffic being the most obvious example – than being in charge of the same pupils within the school gates.

On the buses

In practice, travelling in the company of pupils is less a matter of a teacher's duty of care than of gruelling personal embarrassment. It is not only probationary teachers or student teachers who suffer: any teacher can be faced with the dilemma of deciding whether to take it upon themselves to intervene either on a one-off basis or as a matter of daily routine. The alternative is to ignore any untoward behaviour and then perhaps be seen as abdicating your responsibility as a member of staff. The position will differ according to whether or not you know or regularly teach the children concerned. You have to calculate the degree of intervention which you can reasonably operate and then, importantly, sustain it on a daily basis.

Teaching in some schools is tough enough during school hours and no-one should feel guilty about preserving their dignity in their legitimate to-ing and fro-ing or even for wanting a peaceful interlude between home and school. The behaviour of some children on public transport can be very bad and may be exaggerated in the presence of a new teacher in order to make him or her uncomfortable. No wonder teachers often stay back after school to avoid this! Worse still are the challenges which come from your pupils' friends who attend other schools and over whom you have absolutely no control, a fact that they know full well.

Legally the bus company is responsible for controlling unruly behaviour, thereby ensuring the safety and welfare of all passengers. The school's concern for the overall discipline and welfare of pupils is important, however, as is its reputation, so full cooperation is usually given. Senior staff invariably seize the opportunity to tackle the problem of bad behaviour on buses and are glad to receive information from other members of staff so that they can take action.

Assuming that you are confronted by this problem on a daily basis, what are the practical alternatives? Suffering in silence is not recommended but neither is martyrdom. You should therefore report disturbances to someone at school, probably the deputy head. Rather than moaning, any complaint you make should be purposeful and backed up by evidence, names and dates. This might be difficult if you do not know those involved but your chances of getting anything done are increased if it is seen, both by the senior staff and by the pupils, that you mean business.

Teachers and their cars

In your first teaching post you may drive a car to school rather than use public transport. One of the advantages of this is that you can more easily carry not only piles of marking, but also the posters, charts and other materials which you will have prepared for your lessons. If you work in a school which has a split site, a car may be a necessity though obviously it cannot be made a condition of your employment.

Although LEAs provide insurance cover for educational trips, it would be prudent to arrange your personal insurance cover so that personal business use of your car is included. Local education authorities and schools under LMS are not likely to insure vehicles which do not belong to them but it is surprising how often situations crop up in school where car drivers are pressed into service. It may be to collect a speaker from the station or take a child to 'Casualty'. Before you start hunting for your keys think twice and check that you are covered, whether it is for an official or an unofficial purpose.

My worst experience occurred when I took a group of sixth formers to visit a local newspaper office. Since one of the pupils was on crutches I took her and some others in my car and, having asked permission first, parked in the company car park. On leaving, as I drove off the car failed to clear the horizontal barrier post in the exit and the exhaust manifold was wrecked. I had absolutely no claim at all on the car park owners and felt aggrieved at facing a large bill especially since the damage had only occurred through an act of kindness. I subsequently discovered that it would have been a simple matter to arrange for my car insurance cover to include personal business use.

Giving lifts to and from school can be hazardous. If you have a regular commitment to pick up a colleague it may be a boon to have some company and even petrol money, but there is always the risk that it could become a chore and an additional deadline to be met.

You may have a conscience about passing pupils without stopping to pick them up, especially if it is raining, but think twice before you commit yourself. You may find that you are beset by a daily pang of guilt but this may be a small price to pay for your independence. It might not pay to be too standoffish though – senior pupils seem to be driving impressive vehicles these days and you never know when you yourself might need some help!

Discipline out of school

Sometimes when you are travelling to and from school, you see pupils acting in a way which is either dangerous or offensive to members of the public. Your response will depend on the circumstances. It is obviously daunting to intervene to stop a fight, especially if you do not know the parties involved. Your indignation is likely to get the better of you, however, if you know the combatants. Even so, pause and weigh up the situation first.

If you witness some bad behaviour in a shopping precinct for example, your instinct may be to disappear. You may feel reluctant to associate yourself publicly with the villains, particularly if you doubt your ability to be effective in the circumstances. Remember though that everyone has to be prepared to do these things in the interests of staff solidarity, the maintenance of school discipline, and the good name of the school. Any flouting of school rules outside school such as a ban on smoking can put teachers in an awkward position if they witness the offence. The problem is compounded if parents do not support the school's authority in the matter. Refer any case to your school deputy head and ask for advice. This is better than plunging into a situation which could be hard to handle.

With dangerous incidents, of course, you will need to act at once. At the risk of becoming the school 'supergrass' you should report any example of dangerous behaviour once you have dealt with the culprit. It is more effective to stop a child there and then to point out the hazards 'in situ' of, for example, crossing the road in a dangerous place. There should be a follow-up to reinforce the message, preferably publicly, so that others benefit from the lesson. Any unseemly 'courting' which you observe can be dealt with discreetly. The reputation of the school is increasingly precious in these competitive times and to be jealously guarded by all, so forget any sneaking sympathy you may have for the couple.

In spite of these potential hazards, remember that some of the happiest and most memorable times for teachers are when they are out of school rather than in it, whether it is a simple picnic or a rugby tour. Although initially the organisation requires an effort, the rewards can more than compensate.

CHAPTER 7

Teachers and Pupils

You only have to sit through a school leavers' concert to appreciate the skill pupils have in identifying and portraying the mannerisms of individual members of staff. Even if you are not yourself the victim of a wicked caricature, you will be fascinated at the knowing way in which the pupils will have identified the foibles of your colleagues!

New teachers are objects of great curiosity when the new year starts. Children at every age are deeply affected by the teacher-pupil relationships which develop, initially with the class group and eventually on a personal level. So much hangs on this relationship for the individual child and yet the teacher is responsible for his or her impact on every single one.

For some teachers, the answer is to maintain a distance and thereby aim to operate a fair and impartial regime. Initially for most people this works but inevitably such distance and evenhandedness is modified as teacher-pupil relationships develop individually. Teachers respond to pupils' needs or, equally, are deterred by them, on an individual level and to varying degrees. Inevitably, pupils sense this. Teachers cannot fail to find some individuals more appealing than others, and yet a professional stance must be adopted in order to enable all pupils to be valued and encouraged equally.

In a primary classroom a poor relationship between a child and the teacher can be catastrophic since the contact time is so much greater than in secondary schools. This is not to suggest that secondary teachers have the monopoly of impartiality; in fact, if they are unduly influenced by the views of colleagues, the condemnation of an unpopular child can be reinforced perhaps eight times a day. It is possible, though, for such a child in a secondary school to find someone who sees his or her best qualities, and it is often a new teacher in whom his or her best chance lies since they can provide a fresh start.

Courting popularity

New teachers have a very natural need to be liked and appreciated by pupils. You may have noticed this as a student. Less secure individuals can be vulnerable to whatever action pupils take in order to exploit the situation. I have known students and inexperienced teachers driven to dispensing sweets, merit marks or, most temptingly, early dismissal, in order to curry favour with individual pupils or to survive a difficult lesson.

It should not be necessary to point out to a newcomer that most of all, pupils want well-prepared, interesting lessons conducted in a calm yet purposeful atmosphere to help everyone achieve success. Sadly, although many teachers are fully prepared to deliver excellent lessons in this way, they are often frustrated at the outset by pupils who are not disposed for one reason or another to allow this to happen. If charisma could be learned or acquired, all these problems would be solved. It is worth considering that some new teachers do win the respect and confidence of pupils and that those people would testify that, however effective they may appear, success is not achieved without hard work and continual effort.

Probationary teachers I talk to stress the need to establish firm discipline from the word 'go'. When pressed to explain exactly how, they are less emphatic! Goodwill alone will not do. There are some important points which, as a new teacher, you would do well to heed. Setting aside the wholesale courting of popularity, preferential treatment of individuals will cause resentment amongst the children who are not favoured and eventually embarrassment to those who are. All this might seem very obvious to anyone with clear personal memories of classroom injustices but, under pressure, it is all too tempting for new staff to rely on certain pupils for support and this can develop into favouritism.

Sexual relationships

At a deeper level, no new teacher should be naive about aspects of teacher-pupil relationships which have a sexual element. Superior age and experience as well as a professional duty gives the teacher the responsibility for preventing any relationship or situation arising which may be against the interests of the child. There are prohibitions both formal and informal which schools maintain for the protection of staff and pupils. In some ways these become more urgent for older children yet younger children are also vulnerable and less well-equipped to protect themselves. It has to be acknowledged, too, that there are corrupt teachers just as there are wayward pupils. Sensible staff protect themselves by avoiding situations and occasions which could lead to trouble or misinterpretation and in doing so protect their charges and themselves. Experienced teachers are likely to be sympathetic and to recognise the discomfort and embarrassment which may be felt by young teachers in awkward circumstances. Indeed they are likely to anticipate problems and make arrangements to forestall difficulties for staff. One safeguard is to keep good lines of communication open to colleagues and that includes senior staff.

It is better to air anxieties about pupils who are unduly clinging for example or who seem to contrive situations in order to be alone with teachers. When there is any secrecy or covert behaviour, your suspicion should be aroused. Compromising situations can be seen a mile off, with hindsight, but sometimes it takes an honest colleague to draw attention to what later becomes obvious. I once had to deal with a case where the persistent and offensive behaviour of two determined girls had become a considerable nuisance to a male member of staff who had the good sense to tackle the situation by reporting it before it got out of hand.

Physical contact with pupils

Touching children is a subject which requires not only serious thought but also open discussion. There are likely to be clear instructions issued by your school or LEA which prohibit physical contact with pupils and these must be scrupulously observed. These guidelines will distinguish between touching which is friendly and touching which takes the form of physical restraint.

Teachers' opinions differ. Some insist that touching is part and parcel of the whole range of human communications which are needed by teachers in order to do their job well, particularly where young children are concerned. Others will be wary and feel that, whatever the circumstances, it is not worth the risk of so much as laying a hand on a child for fear of misinterpretation.

Younger children will have a different relationship with their teachers which may well include hugs and cuddles when needed. The disposition of the teacher and his or her particular style of communication will also have a bearing on this. Some teachers would feel inhibited and constrained in their work if they could not respond naturally to the needs of the children in their care.

Children will vary too in their home experiences both in the amount of physical affection they receive (and for that matter in the physical punishment they suffer). There is all the difference in the world between a theoretical discussion on the subject of touching and, in the heat of the moment, deciding what to do. It may be hard to predict the behaviour of a child in a fraught situation just as it may be hard for a teacher to anticipate a personal response.

Under stress, new staff should err on the side of caution. Established staff enjoy the confidence born out of experience and an understanding of the boundaries which apply and are therefore perhaps able to take a more relaxed view. Teachers whose subjects include an element of physical contact such as P.E. and dance may be more poised, being familiar with the limits of acceptability in these matters.

Adolescents may react dramatically to being touched; it can be very intrusive for them and thoroughly unwelcome. I once observed a teenager explode with anger when her hair style which had been ridiculed was then touched. To her this was an outrageous violation. The insensitivity of this gesture added fuel to a situation which had already grown out of control. Trust and acceptability are key factors and if they are lacking, the indignation which inappropriate contact may cause can be powerful. If you sense that this may be the case, make do with a smile or a word of encouragement rather than risk giving offence.

All this may well inhibit a teacher's natural, caring reaction to children but one must safeguard oneself and be reconciled to the fact that in order to protect children who are at risk, it is necessary to impose restrictions on bodily contact with children. This may have to be at the expense of the children who do need to feel the comfort and security which comes from a teacher's demonstration of affection and who are denied it.

Physical punishment

It is easy to recognise the outlawed touching which is included in the category of corporal punishment. We know that it is illegal for teachers to administer physical punishment under any circumstances. This of course is regardless of how often and how heavily the children are chastised at home. While the law is clear about corporal punishment, there is a measure of interpretation when it comes to situations where, for example, children fight each other or inflict injury on themselves and teachers are required to intervene physically.

The D.E.S. has a set of guidelines on physical intervention which should be available in all schools. New teachers would be well advised to take note of its contents.

With the increasing concern that there is now for children who suffer physical abuse, teachers and members of other caring professions are vulnerable to accusations. It has to be realised that children too are aware of this and may exploit the situation.

Dealing with older pupils

Staff new to secondary school teaching may in some cases be very little older than their pupils and in some situations may identify more readily with sixth formers than with older colleagues. However sympathetic you may feel towards older pupils and their grievances, and however much you may feel you have in common, the fact remains that your roles are different and an unbridgeable professional divide exists which serves a good purpose. One practical way in which this distinction can be maintained is for new staff to resist the temptation to make inappropriate disclosures, for example about another teacher, something which is all too easy to do when trying to establish a relationship with a class. Pupils will revel in such confidences and may indeed provoke them. Red herrings provide a welcome distraction and they know well how to flatter inexperienced teachers into showing off or trying to impress pupils in an effort to gain their attention and respect. Although you will want to be friendly with older pupils, you must also act professionally.

Pupils tend to see through excessive chumminess as quickly as they see through attempts to pal up with them by using their slang and their nicknames for each other and it causes embarrassment all round.

In loco parentis

Problems in relationships with pupils can occur, not necessarily through foolhardiness or insensitivity, but when pupils rightly expect help from adults into whose care they have been entrusted. When as a teacher you are *in loco parentis* you are in place of the parent albeit for a limited amount of time. While you may not be an experienced teacher yet, you have received a professional training and were employed for your personal qualities which included a sense of responsibility and a capacity to care. Rather than carry this responsibility too heavily, take a pride in the trust which has been placed on you. Provided you keep the children's interests to the fore you are unlikely to fail them. A teacher who is *in loco parentis* may be the only source of help, protection or advice for a child undergoing a crisis and yet there are certain to be limits to the competence of the teacher, of which the child may be unaware. Even though a pupil's personal disclosure should not be provoked either publicly or privately, there are times when such things cease to be a matter of protecting family privacy and are superseded by the child's needs which take priority. A teacher's job in these circumstances is to be a good listener and to take action.

Pupils' confidences

Children need to be able to trust adults, and though this may lead to an unwelcome burden of responsibility, it can be ameliorated by referral to an appropriate agency. Children do not disclose important information without reason. Sometimes they try to secure a promise of confidentiality: but, if you can help it, never guarantee to keep a confidence, especially if there is a possibility that the law has been broken.

Sometimes children need to express serious anxieties which may be relatively insignificant to an adult, such as an admission in order to clear a guilty conscience. Serious information which they cannot contain such as the disclosure that they have witnessed a crime, can be a grave burden for a teacher and must be passed on in the child's best interest, even if the child's confidence is broken. In your well-meaning efforts to comfort and reassure, you must never promise outcomes to situations of which you cannot be certain. No child deserves to be let down by an adult in whom he or she confides, let alone a child who might already be damaged or upset. Sometimes insensitive adults block a child's disclosure by presenting inappropriately their own experiences in order to demonstrate some fellow feeling. It is better to concentrate on the child's story than on your own.

It goes without saying that all privileged information must be guarded and only used where the child's good warrants it. Occasionally pupils make serious complaints about other members of staff in confidence and this is awkward. A new member of staff may be loath to believe anything detrimental about a colleague, but equally a child's testimony must be taken as worthy of serious investigation. Experienced staff may exercise their own judgement in these matters but newcomers ought to be guided by whoever is appointed to supervise them in their probationary year. One should feel a professional responsibility to be loyal to fellow teachers and not fall into the trap of criticising them, directly or indirectly, in front of pupils. This does not, however, override natural justice and the obligation of care that exists when teachers are *in loco parentis*, i.e., acting in the way that a responsible parent would.

Discipline and new teachers

The exercise of discipline is a major preoccupation of teachers in carrying out their professional responsibilities. It is particularly the concern of new teachers because, not only do you have to consider constantly the maintenance of a fair and workable level of discipline which is in keeping with the school's norms and can be justified as reasonable, but you are actually engaged in the struggle – and it can be a constant struggle – to implement effectively the various rules and standards which the school has set.

Discipline in this context refers to the upholding of an agreed set of rules and the measures which are taken in schools to ensure that they are kept. The meaning of discipline can also refer to such things as the inculcation of values, the promotion of self-discipline and the striving towards high personal ideals. This is a different, but not contradictory concept which represents higher educational objectives. When new faces appear in the staffroom, behind the welcome is always a sizing up on the vital question of whether the newcomer will be able to maintain discipline effectively. Qualifications and career records come a long way behind this question which is both an individual and a corporate concern. Rightly or wrongly, the staff as a whole want to be sure that there are no weak links in their ranks. They will tolerate all sorts of personal failings, absentmindedness, nicotine addiction and so on but an ineffective teacher who cannot control pupils poses all kinds of problems and is a burden to everyone.

On one level, discipline is a school responsibility. The type of regime which characterises the school will be dictated largely by the personal style and standards of the Head who is held to account ultimately. The professional responsibility of an individual teacher is to uphold and support the school system, though of course this will not be done in an exact and uniform way since individual teachers do have a degree of professional autonomy within the system. As a new teacher you will soon recognise the limits of your competence to establish discipline. Some matters will be well within your own personal scope and some things will be quite outside your ability to influence matters. The skill lies in distinguishing between these two and acting accordingly.

It is remarkable how quickly in school the exigencies of the situation persuade the new teacher to seek the solidarity of the staff group in matters of discipline. It soon becomes clear that new teachers are prepared to adopt and uphold all kinds of rules and regulations which may have struck them at first as petty or trivial, in the overriding interest of maintaining a coherent school society.

As a new teacher, though you might not feel that you handle matters of discipline with confidence, at least you can console yourself that apart from the immediate issue, you are not personally to blame for whatever has caused the build-up to the problem. You may have been presented with an ungovernable class which no-one would take on. This does happen to new staff, both experienced and inexperienced, and you should not feel responsible for their previous and current misdemeanors. Your newness can be an asset. For many pupils, you will present to them the possibility of making a fresh start and a chance to turn over a new leaf.

A recently broadcast radio documentary programme included a real example of a student being guided through a lesson which had been marred by pupils' bad behaviour. The striking feature of this was the down-to-earth, practical discussion which took place with the teacher who had observed the lesson. Anyone who has received this kind of help on teaching practice will realise that this is invaluable. It is recognised that students need this help and it is expected to be part of their training and assessment. The position for probationary teachers, however, is somewhat ambivalent. You are caught in the cleft stick of trying to establish yourself as a competent professional teacher and yet needing support to sustain your role without loss of face.

People do not necessarily realise that probationers may be at a low ebb once the first few weeks of term have passed and pressures start to mount up. The honeymoon period with the pupils will be over, the previously planned lessons and projects will be exhausted, and the tiredness and weariness will be harder to shake off. This is compounded by the fact that the rest of the staff are beginning to tire as the most taxing term progresses and their reserves are dwindling, so you may need to take the initiative in seeking support. Try to be constructive about getting help with discipline. You are well advised to get to grips with difficult situations in this testing time and if this means asking for assistance, at least it shows that you mean business and pupils will respect your determination. You might be able to negotiate with a more experienced colleague to have some pupils taught elsewhere for a while until you get to grips with the majority of a difficult class.

It is likely to be much more productive to discuss avoidance strategies with a colleague than simply to drag recalcitrant pupils to be punished by another member of staff who has not previously been involved in the matter. Having said that however, in an emergency you need to act decisively and this may well mean relying on other teachers. You should certainly marshall your resources by consulting an appropriate staff member if you anticipate trouble, and it is therefore important for you to find out at the start what procedures you should follow.

Any information which will throw light on the situation is worth having and this will help you to decide on the stance you intend to take. You should, of course, adopt strategies which pre-empt unacceptable behaviour and so minimise the possibility of confrontation. At the same time, you should not be seen to be ducking confrontation by just ignoring incidents since children will see this as a sign of weakness. If an incident gets out of control, your job is to get help and recover the situation as quickly as possible. You do not, though, have to deal with matters of ill-discipline there and then if it means disrupting a lesson; indeed this could invite confrontation and become counter productive. Say quietly that you will deal with it later, and always do so. The lesson can then continue and you have time to decide what best action to take.

Sooner or later you will discover with relief that it is not vital to be an immediate popular success with the children in order to be a successful teacher.

Administering punishment

If ever you need to know where you stand in terms of your professional and legal responsibilities as a teacher, it is when you have occasion to punish children. As a new teacher you have two competing needs. One is to be given firm, clear guidelines to follow when you carry out any punishment in school: the other is to be trusted with sufficient personal scope to interpret the school rules using your professional skills and judgement.

At college you will have studied many aspects of reward and punishment. You will have considered a variety of approaches based on the different theories of human behaviour and you will probably have debated such things as the moral justification for punishing children, the basis of the authority which a teacher exercises in order to control pupils, the need for whole-school policies for rewarding and punishing children, and so on. In the course of these discussions you will have looked at different ways of imposing discipline, and of course on teaching practice you will have been put in the position of exercising your judgment and your authority as a teacher.

Further light will have been shed on the subject by the teachers you worked with on teaching practice. You will have observed a variety of measures being taken in order to instill the discipline of the school and in the process you will have had an insight into individual attitudes and convictions by hearing teachers justify their actions. Alert students will have observed the reactions of the pupils to their treatment as well as noticing the events which provoked the confrontation. When you see some teachers exercising control, it can seem as natural as breathing. It is not that these experienced teachers are callous and unthinking but simply that they control by communicating the confident expectation that their will will prevail. This comes with practice.

Since when you start teaching you have yet to develop the confident, almost instinctive approach to discipline and punishment of the seasoned practitioner, you will need to look out for other sources of guidance. Remember that your newness enables you to think afresh about how you tackle behaviour problems and to choose which strategies to adopt in order to cope. Older teachers can fall into the trap of dispensing punishments automatically. Children then see this is predictable and, to a certain extent, it lessens the effectiveness of the measure. For a new teacher, it is important to be seen by the children as consistent. The whole structure of authority in the classroom depends upon having an understanding based on mutually agreed (if unspoken) expectations and standards of behaviour. Teachers are responsible for establishing and maintaining this relationship over time and, if all goes well, they will be rewarded with the trust and respect which they have earned.

An obvious guide when you begin teaching is the official school policy on discipline and punishment and the rules which accompany it. Not only does this give legitimacy to your actions but it reminds you of the fine detail, such as the exact number of ear-rings permitted in each ear, which you may have dismissed initially as impossibly petty but which you later may need to quote.

It is important too that this information has been conveyed to parents and that pupils know what is expected of them. It is unreasonable to expect their cooperation without this. Indeed it is extremely important to be conscious of parents' reactions when you take steps to discipline children. Any parent has the right to challenge the way in which their child has been punished and you may have to justify your actions.

For every child who is ashamed of behaving badly and therefore shields his or her unfortunate parent from the distressing knowledge of it, there is one who goes home indignantly and gives a version of the story which presents the teacher in a bad light. It is impossible to predict how parents will react to the way teachers punish their children, though you soon get to know which of them takes an interest in the behaviour of their children and supports measures the school takes. If you act in line with the school policy and take advice from colleagues, you should be on firm ground in matters of discipline. You only risk a mistake if you overreact in a way which is clearly unreasonable.

Oddly enough, the pupils' reactions are a reliable guide to your own behaviour, provided you are not so incensed as to fail to notice them. Children tend to have a highly developed sense of justice and have the advantage of assessing your performance in relation to that of other teachers.

As a rule of thumb I found that it was better to be tough on groups and soft on individuals. That does not mean that I recommend punishing classes en masse. On the contrary, you risk an accusation of unfairness if you do punish indiscriminately, though there have been cases where keeping in a whole class was upheld by a court of law to be reasonable. My point is rather that pupils expect teachers to be firm and welcome a clear sense of direction. Gradually you will be seen to operate your own style as an individual. Your reputation will be established and your tolerance levels will be recognised: as a result the classroom tensions which lead to conflict will be reduced. It is remarkable how sensitive children are to the limits of what each member of staff will tolerate. In order to appreciate this awareness, you only have to listen to them in the corridors hurrying to one lesson and dawdling to another, predicting teachers' reactions.

Misgivings

When you punish children, you often have a crisis of confidence, inwardly wondering whether you are reacting to their misdemeanour in a fair and effective manner. The dilemma may be compounded if you are in a public situation, in which case you are exposed to having your actions judged, not only by pupils but also perhaps by colleagues. This can inhibit your response and make you feel nervous, so act decisively and deal with the matter as swiftly as you can.

Even an experienced teacher, new to a school and yet to internalise the norms and expectations peculiar to that school, is likely to tread warily at first when reprimanding children. Whole-school policies for rewards and punishment tend to create a reassuring degree of consensus and provide guidelines for everyone, though scope for a measure of variation remains. There was a time when Punishment Masters and Mistresses of Discipline existed in some schools. Their job was to mete out the punishments prescribed by other members of staff. Presumably the purpose was to ensure that children were not dealt with by staff acting in anger, but it creates an appalling prospect of the damage caused by misplaced wrath, let alone the effect it must have had on the unfortunate children waiting to get their just (or unjust) deserts.

The legal framework

As a new teacher you are likely to be more interested in rewards and punishment as an aspect of your professional responsibilities than in the precise legality of your position when working as a teacher. In practice you can safely leave the legal niceties to the school management provided you have a general idea of the position. Corporal punishment is now outlawed by Section 47 of the Education (No 2) Act 1986. You need to know the fact but you may never be asked to quote chapter and verse.

In other respects, the law in this area is necessarily dependent on circumstances and incorporates notions of reasonableness and good faith. In extreme cases where accusations are made of excessive punishment, it requires an interpretation on the lines of whether the teacher gave the sort of punishment that a reasonable parent would expect a child to be given.

Individual and practical aspects

The individual impact of teachers' personalities and the quality of the relationships they establish with pupils can have a considerable bearing on the effectiveness of punishments. A look of disappointment from one teacher can be more upsetting to a child than more drastic measures from another. Ironically it is extremely difficult for schools to make absolutely hard and fast rules to govern the administration of a punishment policy, even though justice demands that this is the very area which requires clarity, consistency and uniformity. However well conceived a policy on rewards and punishment might be, it is in its implementation that the problems arise and where inconsistencies can appear.

Even if you lean towards eccentricity, your first spell of teaching is not the time to inflict bizarre or unusual punishments. Your repertoire will probably be confined to the standard school sanctions of detentions and extra work.

Of course, there are practical drawbacks to all methods of punishing pupils. If you set extra work, you punish yourself by adding to your marking load and risk ruining the pupil's interest in your subject by presenting the work in a punitive light. If you detain pupils you have to stay back too unless the school operates a detention rota. You also have to have a sensible regard for the children's safety and travel arrangements, so official notice must be given parents. In spite of all these drawbacks, your prime motive is to underline the fact that you will not brook certain behaviour and that when you threaten a punishment, you mean what you say. Remember, though, that threats of punishment are hollow if you have neither the power nor the intention of carrying them out. Never bluff.

Verbal admonitions must never become sarcastic or personally vindictive. As far as you possibly can, concentrate your disapproval on the deed rather than the culprit. You soon learn when to make general comments and when to target your remarks at individuals.

Children will appreciate it if you can make strong pronouncements to establish control without trapping the whole class into a punishment by a threat which once made, has to be carried out. Your expectations must be absolutely clear and occasionally reinforced with reminders otherwise unwitting transgressions will occur which you cannot then overlook. Better to say something like 'Remember that I said you had to work quietly until lunch time' rather than 'If James speaks again, the whole class stays in at play time'.

Try and think back to how you felt as a pupil. If you remember how boring school can be for some pupils it might encourage you to vary your delivery when it comes to punishment. Even when they are being berated or criticised, pupils appreciate an imaginative turn of phrase and the feeling of being treated as an individual. You can listen to their version of events and still exercise your authority and deal with the matter fairly. You may experience some fellow feeling with the children if you have to suffer a dreary assembly full of interminable nagging about complaints of bad behaviour at the bus stop.

Inexperienced teachers sometimes have problems when they actually hand out punishments. Try not to make it a more protracted business than it needs to be and be quite clear what the punishment is and why it is being given. If you think that you might forget to follow the matter up, make a note of it. Seeing this should impress on the child that you are serious.

A probationer asked me recently whether she really should be spending 60 per cent of her time chasing up missing homework. It may feel like that in the first year but if you persist, life will get easier because two things happen. Firstly you become more determined and effective in your insistance and secondly, the pupils are more used to you and put up less resistance. You need to create the strong impression that you are serious and single-minded in your approach. If you show weakness or indifference, then it might take a while to restore your authority and achieve the cooperation you expect.

Professional priorities

It is hard sometimes to keep to the forefront of your mind that your main purpose in school is to ensure that the pupils benefit from your teaching, especially when your time seems completely absorbed by the demands of preparing work, maintaining discipline, chasing up homework, keeping records and responding to the many pressures, external and internal, which abound.

All teachers can get caught in the dilemma of deciding priorities on the basis of competing needs. What happens, for example, when the needs of an individual child can only be met at the expense of the rest of the class? Experience comes to the aid of old hands when resolving these issues, but new teachers should ask for help on occasions when, for example, parents arrive unannounced or when a child is so distressed that he or she must be heard in private.

In general, never leave a class for any length of time: but if you really must, never do so without some sort of cover and without explaining the situation to another member of staff. Sometimes you are obliged to continue teaching your class while a situation which concerns you is dealt with by someone else, in which case, it is gratifying if your involvement is acknowledged and you are kept in the picture. This, as well as giving personal and professional satisfaction, should be part and parcel of a staff development policy. Your instinct should always direct you to try and appreciate where the needs of the child lie and whether this leads you to back away or to insist on further involvement.

Protecting personal property

You learn the painful lesson of looking after your own property the first time something of yours gets taken. When you begin in your new job, get yourself something like a cupboard, drawer or filing cabinet which locks. Never take money to school in large amounts: in fact don't take anything valuable to school at all if you can help it. It simply isn't worth the aggravation of losing a watch or a good pen when you can make do with a cheap substitute. Some schools have major problems with theft and therefore it is only sensible to reduce the likelihood of becoming a victim. Avoid presenting children with a temptation which they may be unable to resist.

A great deal of time is spent in schools in investigating theft and lessons are sometimes disrupted for this reason. Teachers would rather be teaching than conducting investigations and searching bags, senior staff have better things to do than weighing in with the heavy sermons and distasteful interviews with parents, and Heads hate having to call the police and suffering the ignominy of local publicity.

Beyond the commonsense level of advice to look after your property, there is a much graver issue of general school security. This prompted the publication by the DES of *Security in School* – a management guide, a copy of which has been sent to all maintained schools. It is a subject to take seriously. If you lose a personal radio, for example because a break-in has occured, you will not be covered by the local authority's policies though the LEA may be sympathetic to an appeal. When LMS is in full swing such a matter might be dealt with internally, though in the first instance you should check your own home policy or see whether your union membership has provided this sort of cover.

Related to the disturbance caused by theft is the similar nuisance which occurs when you simply lose your property. If you try and keep your possessions in an orderly fashion, there will be less likelihood of mislaying something vital like a mark book and setting up a hue and cry on the assumption that it has been taken, only to discover it later in a pile of debris. The effect on your blood pressure is much the same whether your property is lost or stolen, and it is equally tiresome for your colleagues who have to suffer the upheaval.

Personal safety

Two recent developments have increased the level of personal protection which is afforded teachers who are subjected to violent attack. Firstly, a change in the law under the Criminal Justice Act 1988 makes it possible for the police to bring prosecutions in the case of assault. Previously, teachers had to bring their own action for assault if necessary.

Secondly, the Health and Safety Commission has warned that legal action will be taken against local authorities who fail to protect the staff in their employ from violence. Teachers can be vulnerable to attack from aggressive pupils as well as aggrieved parents, and this possibility is now being taken far more seriously.

Lending your property

However much you trust the children you teach, and however much you would like to help them with their school work, lending your own property is not a good idea on the whole. It isn't worth the irritation of being without something you need yourself, perhaps having to make repeated reminders and then risking any damage or wear and tear when it is returned. With photocopying facilities more widely available, the need for pupils to borrow books has diminished. You may feel compelled to lend a video tape or some computer software and then live to regret it. Lending school property can be equally nerve-wracking, so err on the side of caution. As a new member of staff you may be regarded as a soft touch compared with your more hard-bitten colleagues, so the obvious thing to do is to refer the would-be borrower to your head of department. If it is a substantial item, do not take it upon yourself to dispense the school's resources without getting someone's permission.

Sometimes colleagues can be an embarrassment in these matters especially when you are given to understand that there is a long-standing agreement that some equipment can be borrowed and you are expected to continue the practice. Remember that such embarrassment can work both ways. You may be putting someone in an awkward situation yourself by asking to borrow a microwave cooker, for example. Perhaps these favours work best on a reciprocal basis, and when you are established as a colleague, you will be able to operate mutually helpful arrangements. However, this reciprocity is less likely to work with pupils because the relationship is on a different footing.

Conclusions

As a new teacher you will probably find that most of the satisfaction which you get from teaching will be derived from the contact you have with the children. Many experienced teachers take increasing comfort from this aspect of their work, expressing their belief in the view that while so much else in education is changing, at least the children are still the same.

Teachers enjoy a unique, privileged relationship with children and although teaching methods change and the curriculum can be altered, the basic responsibility which teachers carry and the duty they owe to those in their care is extraordinarily wide and varied as well as quite unrelenting. Teachers are as good as they give: and what they give, though hard to measure, is easy to recognise. Pupils appreciate good teaching both at the time and later on with the benefit of hindsight.

CHAPTER 8

Professional Development

When new teachers start work it is assumed that they possess certain personal qualities and academic qualifications and that their college course has prepared them adequately for embarking on a career in teaching. Given the right experience and support, they have the potential eventually to become good teachers.

However, the speed at which changes come about, in education as elsewhere, means that a teaching qualification cannot have an indefinite shelf life in the same way that, for example, a driving licence has.

Initially, the skills you acquired during teaching practice will be developed and reinforced through practical experience in school. Gradually the management of classes and of individual pupils becomes easier. Lesson planning, often viewed as an irksome, mechanical exercise on teaching practice, becomes a practical outlet for imaginative curriculum development, given the extra freedom and increased urgency of working in a long term situation. This is all part of a dynamic process which at some point will require topping up and stimulating in order to consolidate what you have achieved so far.

The exact stage at which further professional development is required will vary from individual to individual, as will the kind of help needed. You might well need to find your feet first before undertaking anything like further study, but you may welcome the chance to attend induction courses for probationary teachers.

It is possible that you have an urgent need for help if, for example, you are teaching a second subject which you had not bargained for or have been given a responsibility for which you should be better equipped. The Local Management of Schools arrangements are having the effect of tightening up the financial provision for further training. It is no longer simply a matter of swanning off to the Head for a signature on your application form to go on a course. Even so, LMS does mean that schools have the wherewithal to respond effectively to the needs which are identified both for individual personal requirements and for the building up of the school's professional resources. LMS will also enable school management to provide staff support with imagination and flexibility. In practice this might mean that supply cover would be provided to enable a probationer to benefit from some classroom observation or work shadowing of colleagues.

Looking ahead

When you are appointed it is wise to draw attention to any specific in-service needs which you have in relation to your post. In this way they can be incorporated into your induction programme. Ideally, you will have left college with a profile which outlines your strengths and your achievements. In the process of negotiating this you will probably have identified areas for development and received suggestions for further work. Your school should provide professional guidance in order, again ideally, to build on your expertise and provide opportunities to plug any gaps and enhance the experience you are gaining.

Although a well-organised profession should provide good quality professional development opportunities and wise guidance, you should make it your business to research the possibilities for yourself. After all, you are in the best position to know your own strengths and weaknesses, aspirations and commitments. You are also in the best place to assess whether you want to undertake further study, either for purely personal advantage or for benefits which are essentially for the sake of the school – not that these are necessarily mutually exclusive. You need to decide at an early stage whether you want to extend your subject specialism or to explore new areas. You might look at the cross-curricular themes of the National Curriculum, for example, or your personal interest might take you into areas such as school management or the fields of Special Needs or PSE.

Further study

Every staffroom noticeboard is festooned with information on the many opportunities which are available for further study. These range from school-based in-service sessions to DES residential courses. If you are planning to add to your qualifications or develop an interest for its own sake, the best plan is to take stock when you feel you comfortably can and work out a master plan for yourself.

You must take into account your present strengths, the experiences you are gaining from your current post, areas which you know need to be developed, and if possible some ideas of an ultimate goal at which to direct your efforts. Obviously no one can be that certain of what life holds in store, but you have a better chance of satisfaction if you work out some idea of the direction of your career than if you either drift or strike out in all directions.

Choosing courses

Having considered an ideal career plan, you should then plot the courses which are going to help you achieve it. You should shop around once you know what you need. When resources are limited, it is all the more important not to risk squandering your chances on unconnected courses which do not contribute to a carefully thought out career path. Obviously this is a speculative exercise since you will not be contemplating embarking on an intensive programme immediately but rather exploring what is available. Try and make yourself a coherent package which is compatible with your abilities and aspirations. Exercise discrimination in your choice of courses. Check that the levels suit your needs, whether or not the courses have been validated and by which institutions. Discuss your plans with the supervisor of your probationary period and find out as much as you can about syllabuses and programmes. Nowadays it is possible to build up systematically a series of modules which can contribute to an M.A. for example, a much better plan than accumulating a random collection of courses and activities which lack coherence and which have no real currency as qualification in the promotion stakes.

When considering any plans for further study, think about the institution providing the courses which interest you. You may have kept good contacts with your college and want to build on that foundation in order to further your professional development in a familiar setting. Alternatively, you might relish a change and the stimulus of a different institution. Consider your personal study needs too. By now you should know how you work effectively. Do you need the support of a group, or would a distance learning course such as those provided by the Open University give you greater flexibility? Are your powers of self discipline up to the challenge of working in isolation, or do you need to be committed to frequent and regular lectures and seminars? Although it is essential to get good counselling for your career development, you must sort out much of it for yourself. Eventually you will need to look at the practical issues of how much time you have and how your household will function without you if, for example, you spend your Saturdays at the local Professional Development Centre.

One advantage not to be overlooked in discussing professional development with the senior teacher responsible for staff development at school is that, since funding and supply staff are finite resources, it is essential that you secure their interest and approval for your work. This is not to suggest that you can equip yourself to become a high flyer on demand. Your situation will be viewed in the light of the whole school staff development picture and the needs of the school. There is a return which the school expects on its investment. This may take the form of a teacher undertaking a particular responsibility, passing on information to the whole staff or setting up and running a project. Ideally it will benefit the school to foster the talents of its teachers and sponsor in-service so that the needs of the staff as a whole are also met.

Personal action plans

When there is stagnation in the job market for teachers and promotion prospects are limited, personal and professional development is a vital way of preventing individual teachers from becoming frustrated when their ambitions cannot be realised. New teachers, however deserving and enthusiastic, will probably have to wait their turn for the opportunity to go on courses or obtain grants for further study unless it is part of their induction programme.

If you feel thwarted by this, you might want to take some initiative yourself, paying your own fees if necessary.This not only speeds up the process but it earmarks you as being dedicated and deserving encouragement. There is obvious merit in being prepared to sacrifice your own time and money in order to develop your interests and extend your repertoire as a teacher.

Feedback from courses

You should make a point of preparing a report on whatever course, workshop, or study day you have attended. This has the dual advantage of passing on your comments to the relevant quarters and drawing attention to your virtue! You should do this whether or not you were funded for the activity and whether or not you were asked for any feedback. Apart from anything else, it is a useful exercise to make a summary of your findings and the value you feel you have derived from the activity while it is fresh in your mind. The dissemination needs some care, however. If you are over-enthusiastic, you will alienate colleagues. Spreading the word too vigourously can be counter-productive. Instead you should aim to win over gradually the people who are likely to be sympathetic and build up your support from there. If you go about it in this way, you perform a valuable service by passing on information to receptive colleagues. I am in favour of the Noah's Ark approach which means that you send out staff two by two to go on courses and thereby more than double the value of the benefits gained: they provide each other with mutual support and can present new ideas all the more effectively.

Always store away your course materials, papers, essays and coursework: it is surprising how useful these can turn out to be. There is increasingly a pressure for the evaluation of in-service work; this is understandable when resources are scarce and there is great emphasis on raising standards. The consumers must play their part in this process. It is in the interests of staff to be critical and honest in their reaction to the courses they have experienced. All this is in marked contrast to the sixties when courses were there for the asking and it appeared that no one was particularly concerned about value for money. It reflected too the climate of expansion when promotion was virtually automatic.

You may find that the very idea of promotion, further study and enhanced qualifications leaves you cold at present and that you cannot commit yourself further when you are acclimatizing to the demands of teaching. It may well be appropriate at this stage to develop your teaching skills and enjoy your work for its own sake.

Keeping up to date

Whether you are ambitious or not, it is still professionally useful to keep up a general interest in the world of education which exists outside your school. One way of doing this is to read the *Times Educational Supplement* and the education pages of the *Guardian* (on Tuesdays) or *Independent* (on Thursdays). It is surprising how insular it is possible to become without the stimulus of keeping up with current issues – though with the recent pace of change, some people may be forgiven for wanting to bury their heads in the sand for protection.

Professional journals are invaluable for keeping up to date with subject or other specific developments. As another way of continuing your own involvement in your subject area, you should consider joining a professional association to keep apace with current issues. School itself is a rich and, to some extent unrecognised, source of in-service development outside your subject if you deliberately exploit its possibilities. I used to keep a personal record of my work and experiences and carried out an annual review for myself. This was a useful way of taking stock and planning. It also had the value of setting out and recording the responsibilities I had undertaken in the course of my work.

If you consider your needs carefully, you can observe established staff, evaluate teaching materials, collaborate on cross-curricular activities, all the time extending your expertise and experience without once having to embark on a strenuous course, go cap in hand to the authorities for a grant or find someone to look after the cat in your absence!

Appraisal

Following a great deal of discussion and pilot work, a national scheme of appraisal for teachers has been agreed by the Government. This will form part of teachers' conditions of employment, and will affect Heads and senior staff as well as those who have recently joined the profession. It is envisaged that about half the teachers will be appraised by August 1993 and the remainder by 1995. Subsequently, every teacher will have their performance appraised every two years.

In each school, the Head or senior teacher is to be responsible for appraising staff. Each teacher will be observed on two occasions, after which there will be an appraisal interview and a statement. Heads will also be appraised, in their case, by people appointed by the LEA.

In announcing these arrangements in December 1990, the Education Secretary Kenneth Clarke said that the purpose of assessment would partly be to give teachers an indication of how well they were doing in the job and partly to set targets for improvement. The intention is not to link appraisal directly to salary levels. Performance-related pay, which is intended to reward work of high quality, is another matter. Although chairs of governing bodies will be given the full appraisal report on Headteachers, they will only be able to ask to see the detail of targets set in the reports on teachers.

It would therefore be a mistake for you to regard appraisal as a way of weeding out weak teachers. Rather it is a means to help teachers recognise their strengths and identify their professional needs. In their 1989 report on developments in the appraisal of teachers, HM Inspectorate noted how appraisal in pilot authorities was linked to policies for in-service training, including whole-school staff training days. Appraisal had proved to be a constructive and supportive device for ensuring that teachers were given appropriate curriculum and administrative responsibilities and opportunities for professional development. It had led to improved teacher performance, had helped Heads to set priorities in their staffing policies and had enabled tensions to be brought out into the open and resolved. I am not suggesting that the matter has yet reached a stage of complete agreement but this is a considerable development and all round cooperation is essential.

Women and promotion

Many professional and commercial organisations now operate career break schemes for married women. As a result of the reduction in the numbers of school leavers available for employment, many large institutions are looking at ways of recruiting and retaining women workers instead. However, although teaching is a career which attracts women, it is only now that provision is being made for encouraging them to stay in the profession. If you look at the figures for teachers on incentive allowances, in particular at the ratio of men to women, it is quite apparent that there is a dearth of women in the more senior management positions. Although 80 per cent of teachers in primary schools are women, fewer than 50 per cent are head-teachers. In secondary schools 50 per cent of the teaching staff are women and yet only 20 per cent are Heads. In both primary and secondary schools, women are vastly over-represented on the lower pay scales.

There is no denying that teaching as a career is particularly suited to mothers who want to work while their children are of school age. The hours and the holidays match those of the children but, while this helps, it does not solve all the problems which can be encountered. Women teachers need to feel that they can return to work without having too many practical problems to distract them from doing as good a professional job as they did before they left to have their children. This is an individual responsibility as well as a challenge for employers.

Of the 400,000 trained teachers in the PIT (Pool of Inactive Teachers) the majority are married women teachers with families. The main obstacles to their return are the practical problems of finding satisfactory child care and reliable support when children are ill. More discouraging than this however, from a professional point of view, is the fact that they are frequently obliged to resume work on a low salary point, which is galling for competent women used to operating at a more senior level. This problem is gradually receiving attention and the needs of married women teachers with children are being realised, albeit slowly. Some LEAs have proposed schemes to enable women to have career breaks but ironically these have been undermined by the fact that, under LMS, the staffing budgets of schools are under the control of the governors who may not feel bound to support what may be seen as an expensive undertaking, however laudable.

Jobsharing can work well in teaching and there are many examples of successful arrangements mostly involving women teachers. There are cases too of jobshares of responsibility posts which is an encouraging development. Individual schools can have quite different attitudes to their married women staff who have children. This often reflects the disposition of the Head, who can exercise a certain amount of discretion when domestic crises occur. This kind of understanding is invariably repaid with loyalty and goodwill.

With the changes in employment contracts following the introduction of LMS and the pressures caused by the shortage of teachers in some parts of the country and in certain subjects areas, there will increasingly be more variety in the terms of teacher contracts, giving wider scope for adapting to local needs. There should also be more imaginative possibilities for job sharing and the creation of special arrangements which will tap the available teaching expertise and experience within this particular group which has hitherto been wasted.

Exchanges

At one time ambitious teachers were well advised to include a spell abroad on an exchange scheme in their career plan. Sadly this is less common now though it is still possible. The personal and professional advantages of a stimulating change of scenery are easy to appreciate, but the opportunities are limited and the agreement of a Head may be hard to secure if he or she is being presented with the prospect of a valued teacher departing, to be replaced by an unknown quantity.

Standards of living in host countries vary widely and juggling with exchange rates can form a deterrent for even the most enthusiastic and footloose young teacher.

It would be interesting if exchanges could take place within this country to enable staff to extend their experiences without the upheaval and expense of going abroad. Some authorities do operate work shadowing schemes for staff within the education service. There is a scheme run by UBI (Understanding British Industry) called a Teacher Placement Service which might be worth exploring. It arranges short placements for teachers in local businesses and industries.

With the increasing interest in Europe and the lowering of international employment barriers within the EEC, there is the heady possibility that a constant swirl of teachers might enliven the education scene. At present whatever movement is taking place is mostly confined to emergency schemes for importing staff to areas of chronic shortage in the UK. It is possible to envisage a deliberate programme of exchanges designed to foster closer ties and greater cooperation for the benefit of schools and pupils, but it is also possible that enterprising individual teachers might simply find work abroad on their own initiative. Looking to the future, new teachers without heavy domestic ties and with a lively interest in broadening their horizons would do well to keep an eye on developments on this front.

If I were embarking on a teaching career this September, I would be enrolling in language classes and energetically arranging trips to Europe, regardless of the subject I was teaching. Apart from the fun of it and the promise of what it might lead to professionally, it is vital to keep up the freshness of your interest in teaching by making sure that you continue with your own learning.

CHAPTER 9

Personal matters

Teachers vary, as do other professionals, in the amount of personal commitment which they feel for their work. This can change too during the course of a career. It might be assumed that maximum enthusiasm and energy will be demonstrated in the early stages of a career whereas a teacher close to retirement may gradually wind down. Personal circumstances change, however, and enthusiasm waxes and wanes for a variety of reasons. Women particularly find that the pattern of their professional life with its possible interruptions for child-rearing will be subject to change. Even an uninterrupted career will have its spells of greater or lesser energy and activity. Anyone attempting to sustain the work out-put of a student on teaching practice would be burnt out by the end of the spring term. It can be appreciated, too, that different schools and management styles can bring out the best or the worst in us as teachers. People respond in different ways to their situations and they also make calculations, consciously or unconsciously, about the investment of time and effort they consider their job to be worth.

Until recent times, although not a job for life, teaching has been regarded as a secure profession allowing for a great range of personal involvement. Under LMS, the ability of governors to award incentive allowances and accelerate teachers' progress up the Main scale is bound to have a considerable effect on this latitude since teachers will undoubtedly be evaluated not only in terms of subject specialism and experience but also in terms of overall effectiveness and value to the school.

Self presentation

Of course, job satisfaction is not just about pay but includes your impression of the regard in which you are held by other staff, parents and pupils. It is prudent to be aware of the visible evidence which is sought by pupils, parents, colleagues and employers to gauge the worth of a new member of staff. Initially the most obvious indication of your professionalism will be your appearance. Even the most casual student on teaching practice realises the need to dress for the part. Pupils are undoubtedly affected by the appearance of their teachers and pick up the messages conveyed by dress, as do colleagues and parents.

I think it is reasonable to draw a distinction between personal choice and style of dress, where people's tastes do not necessarily coincide, and the care which people take over the cleanliness and suitability of what they wear. Oddly enough, however, it is often unconventional dress which is a target for complaint while the signs of careless hygiene are overlooked.

You will sometimes be aware of situations where the prevailing dress code becomes a gender issue, if, for instance, it is made clear that trousers are only to be worn by men or that earings are only suitable for women.

Newly qualified teachers are unlikely to be able to afford a very varied wardrobe and, especially if their clothes are likely to be spoilt or damaged, will not be prepared to wear anything other than utilitarian outfits. Schools operate dress codes for staff both formally and informally and generally it is not worth antagonising colleagues by running counter to the regime to any great extent.

Despite this caveat, your dress need not be dull and dreary. The boredom factor in appearance is an important consideration as any parent of teenagers will tell you, so it helps to ring the changes. Again, the way you present yourself communicates messages to pupils, and while you will not be able to camouflage poor teaching with stunning outfits you would probably prefer to look interesting and lively rather than boring and predictable. A very impressive teacher I know says that she dresses for school each day as if an inspector was due to pay her a visit, a sobering thought which for some would constitute self-induced occupational stress.

Should a really serious conflict occur over what you wear for school it might be that this is the tip of the iceberg and there are other issues at stake. Recognise your own paranoia and learn to distinguish between general rules about dress and anything which smacks of victimisation or a personal criticism. 'Power dressing' might help your confidence in the first few weeks and sometimes you can put on an impressive performance if you feel you look the part.

Personal problems

At a recent meeting of headteachers I was startled to discover that money difficulties far outweighed all the other reported problems which probationary teachers faced. This may be due to low pay or it may well happen that the more immediate concerns of teaching result in the neglect of personal financial matters which do not have a habit of solving themselves. It is best to consult someone or at least make your preoccupations known. This might yield some practical help but if not, you still are wise to air your worries.

The Head or whoever is responsible for your welfare may take a personal interest in this or other any problems you might have. However, there are likely to be areas of privacy you wish to maintain and personal independence to be protected. It may be a source of distress and even embarrassment to approach the Head with your financial problems, but at least it is well known that teaching is poorly paid and that others are, or have been, in the same position.

Other personal matters may cause more distress both to suffer and to disclose, but it may be necessary to communicate the problem. Matters usually come to a head at school when you need to ask for time off, to see a lawyer or a doctor for example. It may be difficult to know how much you want to confide. In the event we sometimes blurt out what we later regret or, with hindsight, wish that we had been more trusting. What you tell and to whom will depend both on the relationship you have developed with your Head and colleagues and on the response which you anticipate. Remember that you are responsible for what you disclose. It is also worth considering how much of a burden you wish to be to the rest of the staff. Notice whether there is a generally sympathetic attitude towards personal dilemmas and spare your colleagues every last detail if you can. When you do need to disclose that you have a delicate personal problem in order to obtain leave of absence, it is often possible to say to the Head or other senior colleague, 'I should be grateful if you would treat what I am going to tell you as confidential'.

Personal politics

Sometimes Heads become aware of the political leanings of their staff. Although such matters can be kept entirely personal and private, some teachers wittingly or unwittingly make their views known and some views may be thought to have a bearing on school matters. Obviously the main concern is that pupils might be subjected to indoctrination or undue influences of a political nature. It is perfectly possible to teach subjects such as sociology or religious studies in a way which does not reveal personal views and bias even though it requires skill and maturity to maintain a balance of opinion. While it is healthy for pupils to be exposed to sensitive and controversial issues especially as they get older, it is not reasonable to present them with one-sided views or impede their access to a range of opinions. To do so could inhibit them from developing their own considered beliefs.

The 1986 Education (No. 2) Act forbids the promotion of partisan political views, whether in actual class teaching or by posters and literature. Political bias may be introduced by displaying badges and declaring support of various causes and interests, and in some schools this is outlawed. A professional approach will prevent a new teacher promoting one-sided views on politically controversial issues, however passionately they are felt. Even when a clash of opinion occurs and heated views are expressed, teachers must retain their impartiality and exercise discretion. However, an important distinction can be made between indicating a point of view and deliberately promoting one. The first is educationally sound, the second propagandist.

Political views are most likely to emerge when teachers themselves are involved in union activity in the case of a dispute or disagreement. Pupils are then exposed to the persuasions of their teachers, but it would be prudent to keep discussion to the minimum in these circumstances rather than be accused of influencing pupils inappropriately. In the extreme case of a teacher belonging to an organisation such as the National Front, a Head would be unable to ignore it, but generally politics are the personal concern of the individual provided they are not regarded as infringing basic moral principles or attempting to spread propaganda.

Religious views

In county schools, religious allegiance is an entirely personal matter for individual teachers. Staff in denominational schools are in a different situation and their position will, or should be, made quite clear-cut from the time of appointment. This will apply equally to adherents of the particular religion and to any staff of a different persuasion who are appointed. It is important that you are left in no doubt as to the full extent of what is involved in joining such a school.

Heads of schools cannot insist that staff attend assemblies and no pressure should be put onto anyone who opts out. It would be wise, however, to declare this position and establish an intention to withdraw at an early stage. Assuming that the position on religious assemblies is clear-cut there can be other occasions which have a religious meaning such as ceremonies and festivals where staff co-operation is sought and yet you may have a conscientious objection to attending. A compromise should be possible, but you will need to decide to what extent you are prepared to cooperate. Unless you feel very strongly on the matter, it may be worth joining in order to feel a sense of belonging, and perhaps to satisfy a natural curiosity.

You may find that religious issues have an impact on the school curriculum which affects the content of the subject you are teaching. Examples might be the Reformation in history or evolution in biology. You will have to make a decision as to whether this jeopardises your integrity as a teacher. If your teaching includes aspects of sex education, for example, you must make sure that this accords with the school's published policy on sex education and you would be wise to prepare very carefully. If your religious affiliations require time off, you should make these arrangements in good time, but generally it is unlikely that problems will arise that cannot be overcome.

Schools which have a strong religious tradition can be very appealing to those adherents who enjoy the feeling of solidarity and shared values which this brings, but they can be equally attractive to those who, initially at least, are outsiders. That said, some teachers find any aspect of religion unacceptable and would not consider applying to work in such a school.

Teachers' private lives

New teachers are often advised to try to establish a social life outside school. This is not an easy thing to do when you are invariably left physically and emotionally drained at the end of the day. Nevertheless, activities which demand regular attendance are the likeliest to provide you with a definite escape from routine and regular out-of-school social contacts. So it might be a good idea to join a choir or a hockey club rather than vaguely taking up an interest in modern art, for example.

You will soon know when outside activities start to have a bad effect on your school work, just as you will know when your social life suffers through a heavy workload. You are responsible for conducting your own life, of course, but your employer is bound to be concerned that the children you teach are getting the best from you. What you do in your own time is your own business provided that you do not indulge in activities so notorious that the school is brought into disrepute. The 'powers that be' might look more favourably on a chess champion on the staff than a champion beer drinker, but it is your own concern provided that you do your job as you should.

School teachers may not now be pillars of communities, if they ever really were, but somehow along with all people who are in positions of trust and authority, they are obvious targets for criticism if anything unsavoury occurs. This rarely happens but it is worth mentioning simply to stress the responsibility carried by anyone caring for children. Teachers know that their reputations have a wider significance than the strictly personal and that their private lives therefore need to stay private.

Professional integrity

Your professional responsibilities should be clearly set out and formally understood on both sides. You will develop a clear notion of the areas where you are prepared to exceed these requirements and where you wish to protect other aspects of your life. Although you will be affected by the example and practice of others around you, your own integrity and sense of priority is your best guide. A simple example of this is the extent to which staff are available at home outside school hours. Some people are happy to be telephoned on school business but others prefer to maintain a distance between home and school. You are responsible for the boundaries you set and will reap the benefits or costs of whatever you choose to do.

Any experienced teacher will be able to compile a list of 'do's' and 'don'ts'. The most useful to new teachers are those with particular application to their own school. 'Keep on the right side of Mr X whatever you do' is a typical piece of advice. It usually refers to either the school keeper or the timetabler. This is part of the initiation and is often accompanied with dire warnings and horror stories which may need to be taken with a pinch of salt!

'Don'ts' and 'don't evers'

My list of 'do's' would be a counsel of perfection and entirely predictable. What follows instead is a catalogue of 'don'ts' and 'don't evers'. There is no order of priority.

DON'T be put off by cynics and malcontents in the staffroom. They only want to reinforce their dismal attitudes by recruiting new-comers. Look around instead and observe those who are getting on with their job in a positive frame of mind and would not waste their time or yours by constantly complaining.

DON'T work so hard that you neglect your colleagues as people and fail to make friends. One of the chief delights of being a teacher is the chance to work with fellow professionals and to find friends in the staffroom. I had a rueful moment when leaving a school where I had taught happily for eight years. A colleague remarked that I had only been in the staff room twice and the second time was to announce my departure. Admittedly this contrasted with my arrival in the staff-room earlier that day to generous congratulations, but the truth was that I had gained promotion perhaps at the expense of developing friendships.

DON'T be so independent that you shy away from asking for help. As a probationer, I was advised by a very powerful senior teacher never to admit, in teaching, that there was anything I could not do. That advice, I think was meant to say 'Have confidence in yourself' rather than 'Detach yourself from everyone and maintain a constant image of perfection'. Teaching is increasingly a cooperative activity unlike the days when staff were isolated experts in their own classrooms. Consequently new staff, while being as well prepared and self-reliant as possible, should develop the confidence and common-sense to be willing to share and learn from others.

DON'T get too far behind with your paperwork. When you start in your new post, although there may well be a feeling of massive confusion until you find your feet, initially it will be no worse than when you were on teaching practice. In no time at all you will be swamped with a huge build-up of marking and correspondence which will need to be kept under control so do your best to keep it to manageable proportions. Don't procrastinate. The important thing here is to organise an effective way of coping with it all. Much will depend on where you actually carry out your work. If you have your own class room and it is equipped with filing cabinets and everything you need for carrying out your marking, lesson preparation and administrative work, then you are likely to stay back and work when the children have gone home. Your only problem is to overcome the weary urge to escape at the end of the day in search of a change of scenery or adult company. Working at school like this, you do have the considerable advantage of being able to file away correspon-dence, lesson notes, policy statements and so on as you deal with them and problems of retrieval should not arise as long as you are fairly methodical in your filing arrangements. At any rate it is sensible to prepare your room for the following day before you leave each evening.

You may find it more congenial though, to do most of your work at home. A probationary teacher in my department used to go home and sleep for a couple of hours at the end of the school day to recover before he could face the preparation for the next day. You may well have different coping strategies or more stamina. Marking can be done anywhere, but it is easier to carry file paper home than exercise books. When you plan your lessons you may well need copies of textbooks and resource material so duplicate copies of key works should be available at home.

DON'T leave the preparation of teaching materials to the last moment. It can be enormously frustrating to realise the night before that you have no time to produce a worksheet. One's stress threshold is also lowered by finding out on the morning of a key lesson that the school photocopier has broken down. Anticipating your material needs is not only an essential aspect of professional practice, but saves considerable nervous tension and personal anxiety.

DON'T let administrative chaos develop. It is better to anticipate the need to deal with vast quantities of teaching materials and to devise a system to cope with it. Make sure you obtain a quantity of files and boxes, and develop a clear system of labelling or colour coding. Unnecessary stress can be caused by the loss of some vital document, a letter perhaps, or an essential set of notes or, worst of all, a piece of GCSE coursework so any time spent in preventing a muddle building up is well spent.

The awful realisation that you have thrown away some vital document is a foul experience which should convince you that it is better to hang on to everything despite the inconvenience rather than risk the panic of losing something irreplaceable. The habit of photocopying all important items may not be environmentally defensible but it is fine for peace of mind. The accumulation of too much junk is an easy problem to solve: that is what the long holidays are for after all!

DON'T expose yourself to too much self-disclosure. When you arrive in a new job, especially if you have moved to live in an unfamiliar area, you will obviously take time to get to know people. If you have bouts of loneliness or are rather unsure of yourself, you may be inclined to confide in any friendly person, but be careful in case you bare your soul unwisely. You may not be sufficiently notorious to rate highly on the gossip scale but you must never underestimate the power of human indiscretion.

DON'T ever be guilty of betraying a confidence. When you are more established you will be a valued colleague if you can be trusted not to pass on gossip or generate it. If you are asked to listen to a disclosure in confidence, think carefully before you give such an undertaking. You may become adept at recognising the giveaway lines which begin 'Between you and me . . .', but it is more difficult when it comes from the Head or a senior colleague unless you happen to know that all and sundry have been spun the identical line and that what seemed like privileged information is nothing of the sort.

DON'T discuss the personal failings of colleagues at all if you can help it. 'Do as you would be done by' is the principle to work on. While it can be almost irresistible to share an opinion about a colleague, be careful. These things have a way of boomeranging.

DON'T let people down. If you undertake to tape a T.V. programme, check a book reference or arrange to meet a child to give some extra help, make sure that you do it. You will find in the course of a day that you are inundated with information, messages, reminders and warnings. Unless you are blessed with a prodigious memory, arrange a system for remembering the vital bits. You could write everything in your diary, as long as you can be sure of remembering where you left it!

DON'T ever comment on colleagues when children might hear. What you intend as a purely objective remark could easily be interpreted as a personal criticism. Even when they hear accurately, children need no help from staff in reinforcing their adverse opinions of certain teachers, and such conspiracy, albeit an unintentional one, would be unfortunate to say the least. Any views on parents must also be kept with great discretion. You cannot know what damage may be caused by a casual remark, however well justified. Of course, you cannot be a paragon in all these matters. You would be a pathetic companion if you were so guarded and mealy-mouthed that you were incapable of venturing an opinion. Aim, though to respect people by treating their feelings and their reputations with the care you would have them lavish on yours.

Stress

When I started teaching, a phrase which would rile me more than most was 'Got the 'ump Miss?' That was all it took for me to abandon my habitual calm in favour of insane irritability. The modern equivalent of this calculated provocation is, 'Alright, don't get stressed'. Stress for teachers is inevitable and no one would challenge the fact that teachers as a profession are feeling more pressured than ever and for very good reasons.

On a personal level, stress is an increasingly prevalent experience and these days no one should think they are immune to its effects. Teachers in the past relied on long holidays and the support of colleagues to relieve stress, though there have always been casualties with breakdowns and illness taking their toll. These facilities are no longer enough to cope with the pressures which now need some realistic anticipation in order to be survived. Nowadays scarcely a week goes by without the *Times Educational Supplement* including a letter or article on the subject of stress.

Performance anxiety can petrify new teachers until they find their feet – or their voices. This is something which tends to resolve itself since you get caught up in the activity of the classroom and stop seeing yourself as a trouper putting on a eight matinee performances a day. Operating in a highly charged atmosphere is extremely taxing, and affects even the most placid characters. Sometimes the tensions in schools are almost unbearable, a great challenge for the management skills and steady nerves of the senior staff. You must not forget, however, that they too are subjected to stressful conditions and the pressures which they feel can be passed all too easily to junior staff unless they make a conscious effort to prevent this happening.

Many teachers attribute the increase in the stress which is suffered by teachers to what they feel is a deterioration in pupils' behaviour. Understandably, teachers will explain unsatisfactory standards of behaviour by pointing to a decline in society or the home backgrounds of the children as contributing to the general malaise. This is quite a difficult matter to judge objectively. The Elton enquiry (1988) investigated a build-up of concern based on anecdotal evidence, union surveys and a general widespread feeling of disquiet. It concluded, however, that discipline problems were stressful because of the cumulative experience of fairly minor incidents of misbehaviour and that teachers could help themselves through proactive strategies to reduce stress by pre-empting the most common problems.

As things stand there is no legal basis of a teacher's authority; in fact a teacher's authority is entirely dependent on an agreement between teachers and pupils and is certainly not automatic as any new teacher will testify. The stresses and strains of these potentially tense relationships can be unrelenting, and have to be experienced to be believed and understood. Having said that, it is possible to anticipate problems and take effective preventative action on an individual level and as a staff group.

Change is always stressful and contributes in large measure to the anxiety teachers feel at a time when their practices are more than ever under public review. Although the greater burden of this falls onto the shoulders of senior staff, the 'foot soldiers' will be affected in due course. The speed of change and the many developments which are being introduced into schools creates a feeling of anxiety which affects the atmosphere and communicates itself to everyone. I can remember a head of department a few years ago making a plea for a period of consolidation in order to provide some respite for teachers and pupils as well as creating a feeling of confidence and reassurance for parents, employers and others. The pace since then has accelerated regardless of these misgivings. Reported feelings of being undervalued are now more frequently cited as a source of stress. The elated feeling teachers get when they have excelled themselves may seem sadly futile when it does not accord with a general perception of what teachers do. This drab feeling is reinforced by poor pay which in turn creates the pressures of financial stringency and compounds the overall problem.

Since part of a teacher's professional responsibility is quite properly about producing a steady supply of well-educated school leavers, there are heavy external pressures for the service to produce, for a competitive world, a competent, skilled workforce within the limits of the resources available. Teachers bear the brunt of any dissatisfaction if the products of their labours are found wanting and this is a source of great stress on both an individual and a corporate level. Even if there are extenuating factors the pressures are still felt.

Those with vested interests are obviously the parents, pupils, employers, politicians and people who generally are concerned with the performance of the economy and the state of our society. Recent research has shown that parents have less respect for teachers than a decade ago and that pupils too have less respect for teachers than they once had. Although teachers are thought by some to be less dedicated than they were, this is not surprising since the work has become more difficult and less financially rewarding.

Taking a detached view of stress among teachers, it helps if you can see the extent of the problem and manage to put it into some kind of perspective before plunging into gloom. The anecdotal evidence can feel overwhelming in the staffroom, and recent research findings offer little comfort. You do need though, to bear in mind that some of these reports about unsatisfactory working conditions have been commissioned by unions who have their members' interests at heart, and so, though this fact does not invalidate the evidence, it does not render it impartial. It seems ironic to me that while there is plenty of information available about teachers' stress, with open discussion in the press and elsewhere, there is comparatively little apparent talk about stress taking place in school staffrooms.

Being yourself

It is important to realise that teachers do not all conform to a particular pattern and that there is no blueprint of the ideal teacher.

There are many versions of excellent teachers and your school contains only a small sample. The popular view that successful teachers are just made that way is a simplistic one. Indeed, to describe anyone as a 'born teacher' is really quite demeaning. There are many kinds of successful teacher and somehow to suggest that their results are achieved effortlessly is neither accurate nor flattering. Good teachers are invariably dedicated professionals, enthusiastic about both their work and their children. Many people have the potential for this and achieve it in different ways. Even the popularity factor, which can seem to a new teacher an essential requirement for the job, is earned rather than bestowed by some good fairy. There are many influences which can have a bearing on what sort of teacher you actually become. Much depends, for example, upon the school context itself. The various expectations of colleagues, parents and pupils also have a considerable impact and the way you respond to them will shape your professional development.

Some of the most effective teachers I know are those who display a strong streak of personal independence in their make up. They make sure that they look after themselves; they determine how they allocate their energies and their time, not in a spirit of selfishness but with a sense of control and judgment. The strong characters are those who develop personal integrity and do not have to be at the beck and call of anyone, whether the Head, colleagues, parents or the children. This does not mean being difficult and uncooperative: it simply means taking a responsible line and being your own person. It requires deliberate thought and a consistency which cannot be established from day one. You build up a reputation gradually for being sound and dependable, and then people feel confident in you as a result.

Good teachers tend to be those who get rid of their performance anxiety as quickly as they can. Standing on your dignity can be a real block, and until you deal with it you can never be yourself in the classroom. The self-consciousness that you experienced on teaching practice will disappear provided, firstly, that you are well prepared and know your stuff and, secondly, that you care about the children and are concerned for them more than you are conscious of yourself at the time. You can pick up tips, prepare teaching materials to perfection, arm yourself with a stock of jokes and good one-liners but unless you are the master of your subject and genuinely want the best for your pupils, the magic won't work.

Group support

You tend to benefit more when keeping up your interest in educational affairs if you belong to a group which regularly discusses such
matters. You may have an opportunity, either formally or informally, to take part in a discussion group at your school or local
professional development centre. A formal group might be a working
party concerned with an aspect of the curriculum or a particular year
group of the school. Although such a group will have a specific
agenda, it will also serve as a talking shop in which opinions can be
aired and views exchanged. Often a group with a sharp focus can be
more effective and enjoyable than a discussion group designed to
debate general educational matters, simply because busy teachers
have little time for anything other than very pragmatic meetings in
the course of a normal day. The Elton Report on school discipline
(March 1989) recommended that every school should have an
informal staff support group to share perceptions and develop
strategies about the management of pupil behaviour.

Staff development days are now well integrated into the school
programme and have the dual function of personal extension and the
fostering of corporate staff development. They will doubtless provide
you with much help. In a secondary school, cross-curricular groups
are usually good value, for personal as well as professional reasons
because you then come across colleagues you may not encounter very
often if you are one of a large staff with clearly defined faculties and
departments.

Informally, people gather in staffrooms to chew the fat. In my last
school one distinguished group gravitated to what became known as
the anti-nuclear table. Most staffrooms will have gatherings of like-
minded people who congregate in this way. There is an abundance of
vital, lively-minded teachers who are interested in ideas and like to
talk. If you care to get involved and are prepared to contribute, you
will find this a stimulating feature of your day, especially if the
conversation is removed from the humdrum of everyday school
matters. Never be too busy to get involved in such a group and if one
doesn't exist, don't be discouraged since you will probably find a
kindred spirit somewhere, especially in a large staffroom.

Support groups comparable to the 'Escape committees' mentioned
earlier are flourishing in staffrooms throughout the country and the
benefits they provide cannot be overestimated. They are, in my
opinion, more valuable than a good deal of INSET. Their highly

motivated members show impressive dedication as well as generosity to their colleagues and while Heads may be nervous in case of subversion, any confident Head worth his or her salt knows that a positive, creative outlet is preferable to pent up frustration among the staff.

Specifically social groups sometimes ban 'talking shop' but it is compulsive if you are interested in what you are doing. If you join a group your family may have cause to be grateful that you can unload some of the week's cares where they belong, i.e. at school rather than at home. Again this might be an occasion for you to develop the ideas you have about teaching and your attitudes to your work. You might be the sort of person who needs to express your ideas and thoughts out loud so that you can explore your feelings and make sense of your own experiences. This is particularly important if you have begun teaching in an unfamiliar neighbourhood and are perhaps living on your own for the first time. This might be a considerable contrast to life in college or at home where you may have taken for granted the opportunities to talk.

Personal records

During my probationary year I shared a flat with a fellow student who had the good fortune to work for an excellent head of department. Among her virtues was a punctilious dedication to keeping records of the teaching done in her department. I was introduced to her efficient method of record keeping which was simple and thorough and which, with gratitude, I continued to use for years.

As a year head, I kept a daily log book, not for posterity but for survival. Information overload can have dire consequences for teachers who carry a serious responsibility for people and their problems. It was a valuable aid when it came to writing reports and profiles, providing evidence to substantiate or refute any serious allegations, tracing a pupil's misdemeanours, for accurate case notes and for giving confident authority to reprimands which could firmly be based on the record rather than hearsay – a particularly important point in dealing with matters of discipline when you don't know the people involved very well. Frequently I used to record vital reminders – using the ubiquitous 'post it' yellow squares. An appointment to see a child, for example, or a note of exasperation – 'Anna and

98

Victoria not to sit together next week (or ever again)' – would be stuck in my diary.

There is another use for keeping a personal record. The therapeutic effects of writing a diary about school can be really useful, something which may be hard to believe if you are finding the first year of teaching a struggle. Rather than being a chore, such an activity can be a simple way of privately dumping your most bitter reactions and any outbursts of frustration. It could be the safest and most elegant solution to some of the toughest and most painful times. You can always look at it later when you have become a secure, confident and vastly improved member of the teaching profession.

Conclusions

Writing for new teachers a few years ago, one might have made a passing reference to various occupational hazards in teaching and perhaps pointed out the necessity to strike a balance between work and leisure and to find an outlet for personal frustration such as joining a squash club. Nowadays things are far more serious, and it is necessary not only to warn new staff about the strain they should expect on a day-to-day basis, but also to recommend long term strategies for dealing with stress problems which are now inevitable.

It is important to anticipate problems rather than find yourself in the mire without having any strategies prepared. This advice is not intended to trigger paranoia. It is simply the sort of team talk I give to my students to persuade them to join a group or set themselves up in an activity which will provide them with essential relaxation or distraction, and, most important, to organise it well before September.

In some ways, discovering coping strategies is like trying to find good, impartial financial advice. The point is that you have to work it out for yourself, to analyse your own needs and the circumstances in which you find yourself. You need some self-awareness to be able to take stock of your strengths, the particular hazards of your work and the steps you can take to avoid, or, if that is impossible, to alleviate excessive pressure. It would seem to me just as important these days to manage this aspect of your working life as it is to organise your in-service needs.

Finally, if you have been helped during your first weeks and months, remember how it felt to be a probationer when you see newcomers in the staffroom next September and see what help you can offer. After all, you will be following a fine tradition. One of the attractions of becoming a teacher is that your colleagues are likely to be kind, welcoming characters who are interested in other people and are only too happy to help when they can. That at least has been my experience.

In order to become an accomplished teacher, you have to put your whole heart into it. You must care enough about the children and what you are teaching them to work immensely hard, especially in the early stages. Teaching after all has rich rewards; these are not financial rewards but if you prize personal independence, real responsibility, intellectual challenge, variety, humour, drama and excitement, companionship and a feeling of being valued and of accomplishing worthwhile objectives, teaching is the perfect job for you.

Further reading

Ainscow, M. and Tweddle, D.(1988) *Encouraging Classroom Success*. London: David Fulton.

Barrell, G. and Partington, J. A. (1985) *Teachers and The Law*. London: Methuen.

DES (1989) *Your Pension*. Mowden Hall, Darlington. DL3 9BG.

Grey, H. and Freeman, A. (1988) *Teaching without Stress*. London: Chapman.

Lowe, C. (1988). *The Teacher, The Pupil and The Law*. Secondary Heads Association, Leicester.

Marland, M. (1975) *The Craft of the Classroom*. London: Heinemann.

McManus, M. (1989) *Troublesome Behaviour in the Classroom*. London: Routledge.

Smith, A. (1988) *Starting to Teach*. London: Kogan Page.

Stock, B.(1991) *Health and Safety in Schools*. London: Croner Publications.

Index

accidents 10, 75
Acts of Parliament: Criminal Justice
    Act (1988) 70
  Data Protection Act (1984) 34, 41
  Education Act (1986) 36, 67, 86
  Education (Teachers Pay and
    Conditions) Order (1987) 4, 9
  Education (School Records)
    Regulation 1987
  Education Reform Act 1988 7, 36,
    38
  Employment Protection
    (consolidated) Act 1978 7
after school activities 47
AMMA 13, 14, 16
A.O.T.s (Adults Other than
    Teachers) 35
appearance 84
appraisal 4, 78
assemblies 87

before school 43
being yourself 94
break duty 10
buses 57

charging 44
colleagues: getting on with 23,
    discussing 91
contracts 4–9
courses 73, 75, 77
courting popularity 56

discipline 60–68, discipline out of
    school 52
  new teachers and discipline 61–63

disputes 14
directed time 4, 20, 24, 44
dress 84
D.E.S. 40, 59, 75
duty of care 49, 50

E.E.C 81
Elton Report 93, 96
'Escape Committees' 3, 96
exchange schemes 81
extra-curricular activities 20, 26, 48

first appointments 1
fixed term appointments 2
further study 74, 75

group support 96
GCSE 44, 91

health and safety 9
home visits 34

induction 25, 73
initial formalities 7
initial teacher training 1, 19, 25
in loco parentis 11, 60
in-service 5, 76
interviews 2–4

job description 2
job sharing 80
joining the staff 19
joining a union 13

keeping control 64
keeping up to date 77

leisure 98
legislation 67
lending property 71
Local education authority 1, 36, 45, 51, 80
Local Management of Schools (LMS) 4, 7, 37, 70, 74, 80, 83

morale 15

NAS/UWT 13, 14, 16
NAHT 13, 14, 16
National Curriculum 3, 74
NUT 13, 14, 16

older pupils 39
out of school 43, regulations 46

Parents 29–42, contacting parents 4, 32, 33
  interviewing parents 33,
    parents access 34
  parents in school 35,
    parents meetings 30
  parent governors 36,
    reports to parents 38
  parents and governors 36
Parents Associations 37
Parent/Teacher Associations 37
P.A.T. 13, 14, 16
P.I.T. (pool of inactive Teachers) 80
pension schemes 6
performance anxiety 92, 95
performance related pay 79
permanent appointments 2
personal matters: politics 86,
    privacy 21, 83, problems 85
    property 69, records 97,
    safety 70
physical contact 57
physical punishment 59
probationers: assessment 27, 28,
  on outing 43, 45

professional development 26, 69, 73, 74
professional priorities 69
promotion 2, 77
pupils: privacy 22, files 39,
    confidences 60
  records 41, punishment 64–67

Records of Achievement 40
Regulations 5
religious affiliation 87
residential school journeys 47

school governors 4, 7, 36
security 70
sex education 87
sexual harassment 24
sexual relationships 15
SHA 16
staffrooms 19–24, relationships 15
staff training/development days 79, 96
stress 25, 58, 92, 98
superannuation 6
supervision 10

Teacher Placement Schemes 81
teachers: private lives 88, union 13,
    teachers and their cars 51,
    teachers and parents 29
    teacher–pupil relationships 55–72
teaching practice 73
Times Educational Supplement (TES) 3, 13, 78, 92
Traveling to and from school 50

Union politics 17
union services 7, 15

women and promotion 79
working abroad 81